51 Shades of Online Dating

A Guide for People over 50

Sandra Lindberg

BookLocker
Saint Petersburg, Florida

ISBN: 978-0-578-63199-8

Published by BookLocker.com, Inc., St. Petersburg, Florida.

Printed on acid-free paper.

BookLocker.com, Inc.
2020

First Edition

Disclaimer

This book is a work of non-fiction. Unless otherwise noted, the author and the publisher make no explicit guarantees as to the accuracy of the information contained in this book and, in some cases, names of people and places have been altered to protect their privacy.

This book details the author's personal experiences with and opinions about online dating. The author is not a licensed doctor, psychologist, or therapist.

The author and publisher are providing this book and its contents on an "as is" basis and make no representations or warranties of any kind with respect to this book or its contents. The author and publisher disclaim all such representations and warranties, including for example warranties of merchantability and relationship advice for a particular purpose. In addition, the author and publisher do not represent or warrant that the information accessible via this book is accurate, complete, or current.

The statements made about products and services have not been evaluated by the U.S. government. Please consult with your own legal, accounting, medical, or other licensed professional regarding the suggestions and recommendations made in this book.

Except as specifically stated in this book, neither the author or publisher, nor any authors, contributors, or other representatives, will be liable for damages arising out of or in connection with the use of this book. This is a comprehensive limitation of liability that applies to all damages of any kind, including (without limitation) compensatory; direct, indirect, or consequential damages; loss of data, income, or profit; loss of or damage to property and claims of third parties.

You understand that this book is not intended as a substitute for consultation with a licensed medical, legal, or accounting professional. Before you begin any change in your lifestyle in any way, you will consult a licensed professional to ensure that you are doing what's best for your situation.

This book provides content related to dating topics. As such, use of this book implies your acceptance of this disclaimer.

Acknowledgments

Writing my first book was a personal goal. It would never have been possible if it wasn't for the patience, knowledge, and support of the many people in my writers group. They listened and offered fantastic feedback. I offer all of you my humble gratitude.

I give a sincere thank you to my sister Deb for proofreading my first raw draft and friend Barbara for proofreading the final manuscript. Thanks to my editor for his critical eye.

The support and encouragement of my friends and family was priceless. Also, thanks to all the people who responded to my online dating survey and to my friends, who shared their stories. This was quite the journey!

I apologize for any typographical or grammatical errors that you will surely find in this book. Kudos to you!

Author Biography

Ms. Lindberg has an MA in Training and Development and is a retired corporate trainer, an artist, and now...an author. She is a mother and grandmother.

Before retiring, she spent years in corporate training traveling the U.S. Not much time was available to cultivate love interests. Upon retirement she used internet dating sites more extensively and has accumulated over 12 years experience with cyber dating. Her experiences ran the spectrum as her stories and lessons learned will tell.

This is Ms. Lindberg's first book and she has learned a lot from her writing journey. She hopes to help others navigate this virtual world and learn from her personal experiences and research.

51 Shades of Online Dating

A Guide for People over 50

Table of Contents

Introduction

> "Online dating is the microwave version of relationships and I'm the underdone burrito with an icy center that nobody wants."
>
> Shani Silver, Guest Writer for the *HuffPost,*
> *February* 18, 2018

Is this you?

There are many people looking for a partner using online dating sites. You are not alone!

This book can serve as a guide, using my experiences to make your love life more successful.

Online dating works for many, but it takes perseverance, patience, a very positive attitude, and a little bit of luck. However, your personal interests should continue being developed and enjoyed, keeping you motivated and loving life.

Many people have met their partners online and are happily spending their lives together—good friends of mine, my daughter, friends of friends, parents of friends, and so on.

Once you finish this read, you will probably make changes to your pictures, profiles, and/or reread your messages for tone and word choices, so you have a better chance of finding your partner. This book will help you create an effective profile and photos to attract the kind of mate you are looking for. You will laugh, cry, and ultimately feel wiser after reading about the author's *real* experiences and lessons she learned.

You will learn there are people who aren't who they pretend to be and people who take advantage of your vulnerability. This book will help you spot that kind of imposter and help prevent you from being victimized.

Knowledge is power! This book should enhance your online dating journey. It should help you determine your likes and dislikes to help in your search. With the methods detailed in this book, you can create a basis for highlighting yourself as a person worthy of the kind of partner you desire and deserve. You have choices and should never be made to feel like you don't.

1. The Generation Over 50

Where did the years go? When I was younger and in a different era, it was easy meeting single men, striking up a conversation, and dating. Well, sorry to say, older single people today have a really tough time meeting the right partner, someone who shares similar likes and dislikes and who really wants a meaningful, long-term relationship where both feel mutual chemistry.

Having been married twice—and then remaining single for many years—my hope was to find someone with whom I can spend quality time and enjoy a movie or dinner. Meet someone who makes me laugh and with whom I can talk about life over a cup of coffee or a glass of wine. Someone to enjoy activities with me, travel together, and share some romance. Sounds easy, doesn't it?

I'm not saying I haven't met and dated nice men. I just haven't met *the one* with the complete package *I* am looking for. Let me share a story of when I thought I found *Mr. Right. Yes, I know…there is no such thing.*

NOTE: All writings pulled from the internet or conversations in quotes are expressed verbatim, with original spelling and grammar.

> **Dr. Fool-Me Mitch**
> *While at my summer place in Minnesota, I met a semi-retired doctor online who lived on the same chain of lakes where I lived. We hit it off the first time we met. I felt the chemistry right away. While he was talking, I was thinking that I wanted to just*

lean in and kiss him. Wow! That is a rare emotion—one I hadn't felt in a very long time.

We spent three fun months together boating, laughing, enjoying bonfires, and taking pleasure in each other's company. We were making long-term plans for spending our winters in Florida, where I lived. He would fly to Wisconsin one week a month to work and then spend the other three weeks with me in sunny Florida. Summers would be spent in Minnesota. I would rent out my lake place to be with him. Sounded like the perfect scenario I had been looking for.

Then, the summer came to an end, and I drove back to my southern home. I anticipated Mitch's upcoming visits. I was more excited than I had been in a long time. My Florida friends were anxious to meet this new guy in my life. The week before leaving, I felt Dr. Fool-Me was acting a little off. I thought he was just sad over our upcoming separation. We had made plans for him to come down in a couple of weeks to check out where I lived. We chatted on the phone every day on my drive home.

Upon returning to Florida, days passed without hearing from Dr. Fool-Me, even after I sent several texts. Finally, I received his response:

"I am glad you had a safe journey back to Florida....I must tell you that I need to pray to God and get his guidance as to whether our long-distance relationship is going to work."

What? You have got to be kidding me. He seemed okay throughout all our talks about how we would handle the arrangements.

> *I responded, "Really? We discussed this at length all summer and you seemed very much okay with everything. Well...you let me know what God tells you."*

> *Several days passed without hearing back. So, I texted him. "Mitch, I have been waiting to hear what God told you to do about our relationship."*

I must admit that I was being a little sarcastic, because he was hiding behind religion for his decision. In hindsight, I probably should have called him on the phone, but I was a bit afraid of what he might tell me, and I didn't want to react on the spot or sound hurt.

Finally, Dr. Fool-Me Mitch sent his reply:

> *"I have decided that I am not interested in a long-distance relationship."*

That was it. No valid reason and not even a personal phone call from someone who had become very close to me. He had sounded so positive about our relationship. I was upset most by the wording being so matter-of-fact and the very crude delivery method. I was hurt and disappointed, but surprisingly, not devastated. That's when I knew I had started growing the outer shell of an armadillo.

Do you know the sad and crazy thing? I really believe the reason our relationship ended was because I couldn't keep a pet at the time, since I was renting a place that wouldn't allow any pets. Dr. Fool-Me's golden retriever was his best friend. He had suggested I find a pet-friendly place, but that would have cost me another $500 per month. No offer came from him to pay that difference, and I didn't think it was my financial responsibility to add that expense for such a new relationship. Plus, it wasn't my dog, after all. So, I told him it was too soon to make such a big change in living arrangements, and I had reasonable rent where I was living. Guess a dog won that love contest.

Funny thing...two months after Dr. Fool-Me Mitch ended our relationship, I decided it was time to stop renting and purchase my own home again. I bought in a community where pets are allowed. Actually, I think God helped *me* in this case, and now I have a furry partner of my own.

Lessons Learned:
- Give yourself a reasonable amount of time to determine if the new person in your life is actually committed to a long-term relationship with you.
- Don't make any major decisions in your living arrangements or other important decisions until you are sure the other person is solid in their plans. A change that decreases your financial health needs special consideration.
- If pressure is being put on you to make major decisions early in a relationship, the "caution light" should be blinking.

Many of my friends have given up looking for a partner in life. Keep in mind, many of us mature seniors have been single for a long time and have become accustomed to the solo lifestyle. This admittedly has some nice bonuses, such as making our own decisions and to come and go as we please. It's important to know what you want and don't want in a relationship—*regardless of what our kids or friends think is best for us.*

Also, for us mature singles the traditional relationship is a thing of the past. Now that we are older, with grown children, and we've probably been married once or twice, or widowed—that makes our needs different. *Wait*...actually, many of us still have *some* of the same needs we had in our twenties. I can surely speak for myself. There may be snow on the mountain, but there's still fire in the furnace, as they say!

Many of us may have forgotten how to date or even flirt. When you find yourself among the *single* population again, most experts say that living alone for awhile can be a good thing. It gives you a chance to get back on your feet and figure out who you are and what you want in your next relationship. You may want someone in your life immediately. If so, ask yourself this important question: Is that desire coming out of loneliness? Poor decisions can be made because of that very reason, as you will learn more about in this book.

There is a big difference in the activity level of the older population today compared to our parents 'era. Today's *silver* population is much more in tune with health and wellness than our parents. We are more active in our retirement years and have the means and time to join the gym, travel, and live in 55+ communities, where there is always a lot going on. There are cruises for singles over 50. Every type of card game, exercise, and entertainment imaginable is offered at clubhouses and community rooms. Free Silver Sneakers—a Medicare benefit— makes it easier than ever to stay fit. We are living longer and having fun doing it. I really like the senior discounts offered on movies these days! *Is going to the movies exercise?*

More members of the older generation are gravitating toward the "single" activities of volunteering and other social events compared to the 1950s-to-2000 era. A social change has taken place.

Online dating has become the way to meet someone while sitting in our recliners with no makeup and frizzed-out hair.

I have been on and off many dating sites for so many years that I've lost count—Match, Plenty of Fish (POF), Date A Golfer, eHarmony, Tinder, Our Time, and a couple others that I can't recall. I'm still an optimistic person. I believe there is someone out there who wants the same things I do and will still appreciate a partner who has all of my qualities…even over 50 (or 70!).

I conducted an online survey with 40 men and women over the age of 50 who were known online daters and asked them a number of questions. One question was, "What was/are the positive aspects of your online experiences?" Below are many of their answers:

- I met nice people who just didn't fit what I was looking for.
- Tried a bunch of new restaurants
- Went to all the theme parks
- Learned more about myself
- I met dozens of great women all across the country.
- Met and have dated someone for over 10years
- Got married
- Broke my boredom
- We will be celebrating our 10th wedding anniversary soon.
- Awareness

These are all great responses, and several of their online dating experiences resulted in marriage or long-term relationships.

Another question I asked, "What was/are the negative aspects of your online experiences?" Below are *their* answers:

- Too many older guys looking for younger women
- Fruitless, having to repeat the same Q & A over and over

- Too many scammers online now. I don't feel I can trust what anyone says.
- There's no spark on the first date—that takes time to develop.
- It's like a job.
- Meeting someone and liking them, and then never hearing back
- It was addictive and too easy to cheat and/or be cheated on.
- Being subjected to strange people
- Loss of faith in men's ability to be forthright
- Lying
- Waste of time, never matched
- Some women are just looking for friends; many lie!
- Fake pictures or pictures of them from 20 years ago
- They lie about their careers.
- They try to get money out of you.
- Took too much time responding
- Men are just looking for sexual encounters.
- On a first meet, the guy felt we should get married because he thought I was a smart businesswoman. He felt that was the best basis for a good marriage. I turned him down.
- Three different guys tried to get money from me.
- The older the guy, the younger the women they are looking for
- I met two men—both seemed very interested and, in fact, had pursued me. We had really nice times together, and each expressed an interest in seeing me again, and then nothing.
- I fell deeply in love with a woman from Dallas. I inadvertently discovered that she had numerous screen names and many male suitors like me.
- Much younger men wanting to hook up with older women
- A first date was made to go golfing, which I thought could be nothing but light and pleasant—a non-threatening situation. At the end of the date, while putting our regular shoes on, my date suggested we go for a drink at the 19th hole. As I considered this, he said, "Since we are in my home territory,

why not go to my house and shower up to get cleaned up before getting a drink?"
- Lied about the most basic information and displayed old pictures
- Online description didn't match individual
- Having to tell them you're not interested after a couple of dates
- I found that guys wanted to write and write.

This survey question obviously triggered more negatives than positives. My book will explore both sides of online dating.

2. Online Dating

There are more single adults in the United States than ever before in history. According to Statista, there are approximately 36.48 million single-person households in 2019. Single people make up the majority of the American population with metro areas in the east favoring women and in the west favoring men age 20-64 (*City Lab, February, 2019*). Single women age 50-59 are the overwhelming majority across the United States. By the time we reach our late 50s and older, the ratio of single men to single women drops because women tend to live longer. *In certain places, it could be a wrestling match over the partner you want!*

To help the single population, the first online dating site, Match.com, was registered in 1995. According to Forbes, in 2018 there were 2500 dating sites in the United States alone and over 8,000 worldwide (www.DatingNews.com). There is a dating site for everyone imaginable.

According to the Pew Research Center (February 6, 2020) 30 percent of U.S. adults say they have used a dating site or app. Their data shows that of people over 50, 32 percent have used a dating site or app. Of those, 12 percent have married or been in a committed relationship with someone they met on a dating site or app. Data varies by the source.

The top ten most popular online dating apps in the U.S. as of September 2019 totaled 219.48 million users according to Statista. Keep in mind that many people are on multiple sites simultaneously. *I'm sure they think it will up their odds.* The bottom line is that there are *millions* of people using online dating in the world.

EHarmony reports that on their dating site there are more men users (52.4 percent) than women (47.6 percent). Is that because men are more willing to take the risks required by this way of meeting someone? *I have my own ideas on this question.*

Statistic Brain Research Institute (June, 2020) reports that 1 in 5 relationships—and a little more than 1 in 6 marriages—begin online. They also report that about 17 percent of marriages and 20 percent of relationships begin online. Online users that have been in a committed relationship with or married someone they met online was at 39 percent in 2019 (*Statista, 2020*). Again, statistics vary by the source.

ConsumerRankings.com has their top five senior dating site picks for 2020 as Zoosk, Our Time, Elite Singles, Silver Singles, and eHarmony, in that order. According to DatingAdvice.com, the top three sites with the highest success rates in ranking order are Match, Elite Singles, and eHarmony in 2020. Elite Singles is another highly rated site for seniors. I suggest you do your research to see which site(s) you think will bring the best results. If you don't like one, try another.

It has become more acceptable in this day and age to use dating sites. In fact, dating online is now the most used mode of meeting a partner. If you wish to seek out other alternatives for meeting that special someone, check out Chapter 27.

In the U.S. alone, the online dating industry is estimated to be worth over $2.5 billion. It's expected to maintain a continuous growth rate of 3.9 percent till 2022 (*Statista*). It's a *very* lucrative business!

Check out the article, "The Best Dating Sites for Older Adults Looking for Love Later in Life," on *Woman's World* (www.womansworld.com) for a lot of information on the many dating sites for the over-50 age group

Some general online dating information compiled by Dating Sites Reviews (datingsitesreviews.com) gives some interesting data:

- 7 in 10 couples found each other online and not in real life
- 75 percent of singles would rather meet their match in real life than on a dating site.
- The global dating market is expected to surpass $8.4 billion by 2024. *Whoa! I need to think about starting a dating site.*
- In 2018 dating apps saw their collective user base grow by 6.5% to 25 million. This year it is expected to be lower at 5.3% increase.
- By 2022, it is predicted that dating app growth will slow down to only 2.2% for a total user base of 28 million.

I think you've had enough statistics. There is so much information available on the internet about online dating, that it can be overwhelming. For more interesting information, check out https://www.datingsitesreviews.com

Online dating may now be the modern and acceptable way to meet a potential partner, but it has plenty of cons to go with its pros. At first you may get a lot of people sending you messages, which makes you feel good. It can also be a painful experience if you don't like rejection, and who likes rejection? There would be less pain if everyone was honest, sincere, and just good people looking for a meaningful and rewarding relationship. Unfortunately, this is not the world we live in today. There are always those who don't abide by the social rules of conduct

When someone asks me, "How long have you been on this site?" How should I reply? If I say, "On and off for over 12 years," they might think, *She just wants free dinners,* or, *There must be something really wrong with her.* Surely, that can't be! Therefore, I answer vaguely, "Too long."

My daughter found her boyfriend of 10 years after only communicating with three or four men. Are there any guidelines as to how long it should take someone to find that special person? It takes whatever time it takes. It's similar to winning the lottery. How many tickets do you have to buy to win? Online dating takes an abundance of patience and energy.

3. Success Can Come in Many Forms

Al, The AC Guy
My air-conditioning (AC) guy was the first person I met who told me about being an online dater while he was fixing my AC one day. The next time he came for my AC checkup, he had found someone. At first, he said he wasn't very interested in the woman he was in contact with, but the longer they communicated on the phone, the more attracted to her he became. They communicated for several months before actually meeting. She lived an hour or more away but eventually moved to his part of town. He has since gotten married, sold his business, and they are now traveling together. He has a great sense of humor and "the gift of gab." I am so happy for him.

Love-at-Last Barbara
Barb, divorced 35 years, is a very good friend of mine. She decided to subscribe to Match.com, and after a couple months of being on this site, she started dating Bill.

After seeing each other a number of times over the next month or two, Barbara grew frustrated. Bill hadn't even tried to kiss her yet. She wondered if their relationship was going anywhere. Was she just wasting her time? Barbara came right out and asked him (she just takes the bull by the horns). It turned out he was quite interested but didn't want to appear aggressive. He was a widower for only one year and new to the dating scene. Once they talked this through, their relationship grew deeper.

In nine months they married (no, she wasn't pregnant). After more than 10 years, they are still very happy and enjoying a nice life together. He's had some illnesses, and they have had life issues to deal with, but they have worked through them side by side every step of the way.

This is an example of the *power of communication*. If Barbara had never approached Bill about her concerns, she could have dismissed him, and their relationship might never have been. *And I wouldn't have Bill to beat at card games.*

Fishing Apprentice Cindy
Cindy has been on and off online dating sites for several years and has dated a number of nice guys for short periods of time. When I asked her what she liked about her online dating experiences, she replied, "I really met a lot of nice guys, and some have become good friends, even though they weren't long-term relationships. There was one nice guy who taught me how to fish. It was a great experience for me because I learned so much from him and really learned to enjoy the sport of fishing. For that, I'm grateful."

"I dated another man for awhile. It didn't work out romantically, but we have stayed friends as dance partners. We both really enjoyed this hobby, and we always know who to call if we want to go out dancing."

Cindy isn't on dating sites currently but viewed her online experiences as learning opportunities. She has a great attitude about what she gained rather than dwelling on any negatives. She's dancing more than ever and loving life.

Two Peas in a Pod
Elaine and Ken met on Plenty of Fish (POF). Elaine had been on this site for three years with little success and Ken for eight years with the same results. Elaine shared that the men she met seemed to be only after one thing (She didn't say what that was, but I'm sure I know). Ken said that he met mostly "gold diggers."

Elaine was attracted to Ken because of his smile. He thought Elaine was sassy, and he liked that. They both said the attraction was immediate, but it took awhile for the relationship to develop. They have been together for over eight years now and have purchased a home together. They aren't afraid to show their affection and appear to really enjoy one another's company. Yes, Elaine is sassy, but in a fun way, and she's not a gold digger— unless she's doing some treasure digging in her backyard.

Elaine and Ken's recommendation for others looking for love online is to communicate for awhile on the phone, text, or by email. That's what they did for several months before actually meeting. They also recommend "not to get too caught up in love aspirations, and keep your common sense and practicality in check—no one is perfect."

I would say Elaine and Ken definitely had *stick-to-itiveness* to stay on this dating site for three/eight years before finding one another. *It's been well over 10years for me, and I'm still sticking to it. I must be like goo by now!*

Didn't Give-Up Don

Don, a relative of a friend, went through a divorce and decided to try online dating. According to my friend, he was a serial dater for several years before he finally found someone he really liked. They moved in together and even purchased a home. That didn't work out the way he had hoped and, before long, he was single again and back on the dating sites. He would date for awhile and move on to the next one, trying to find the right person for him.

Then he met someone with whom he really clicked. She was a business woman, was very independent, and had been single for some time. They have now been married for more than a year and are reported to be very much in love. They are both allowing each other to continue the things they enjoyed doing before they were married, while still truly enjoying each other's company.

Here is an example of two people with few activities in common and who are both very happy because they are allowing each other the independence to be their own person. According to Don, what attracted him to her was that she was a smart business owner, just as he was, and that she was a busy person and wouldn't be dependent upon him to entertain her.

Other Success Stories:

Four people in my writers' group met their spouses through online dating sites. One met his wife in a

> *chat room and has been married more than16 years. They all report they are still very happily married.*

These scenarios prove that online dating success can be measured in a variety of ways, and not always by finding the *person of your dreams.* Perhaps it's enough to find good friends and learning something new from others' experiences, along with finding out more about yourself and what you want and don't want out of life. Every relationship, no matter how long or short, is a learning experience.

There are many people I know who have found their *match,* which is the goal shared by everyone who is seriously looking for their partner on these sites. They know it can work. It just works faster for some people. Sadly and understandably, many people give up before they are successful.

Whenever I tell people that I'm writing a book on online dating, they tell me they, or someone they know, met their spouse or partner online. These stories are everywhere!

Lessons Learned:
- If you are interested in someone, but are bothered by something they did or didn't do, communicate openly with them about it.
- Don't discount someone if the sparks aren't flying in the first few conversations. Keep talking, because they may surprise you.
- Don't give up if you have a slow start in meeting potential matches. Things can improve.
- You don't have to be a perfect match in all areas. Be okay with letting your potential partner be who they are. Enjoy each other's independence.

4. What are People *Really* Searching for on Dating Sites?

Below are some responses to this question based on the online survey I conducted with a sampling of people over 50.

- *Just looking*
- *Long-term relationship*
- *To meet potential dating partners*
- *It's a way to meet new and different people.*
- *It would allow more opportunities to meet someone.*
- *To find a comparable mate*
- *To date a golfer*

Of those who responded, 73.6 percent were still looking.

Most online dating sites ask profile questions when signing up and setting up your profile. For example, Plenty of Fish (POF) asks the following questions:

1. I am seeking a (choose man or woman)
2. For: (choices are):
   - *Hang out*
   - *Long-term*
   - *Dating*
   - *Friends*
3. Intent (choices are):
   - *I am serious and want to find someone to marry*
   - *I want to date but nothing serious*
   - *I am looking for casual dating/no commitment*

- *I am putting in serious effort to find someone*
- *I want a relationship*

There are some fuzzy lines between several of these choices.

In my opinion, online daters can be separated into 11 different reasons or motives as to why they are using online dating sites— *regardless of how they answer.*

1. *Serial Dating.* This is the person who just wants a social life and something to do on the weekends or when they are bored. This motive can mean several things. It could mean you probably aren't looking for anything long-term or serious. It could mean sex as the end goal, with no attachments. It could mean that you are building your career and don't have time to cultivate a meaningful relationship but still want to date occasionally. It could also mean that a person wants to test the waters to see what's out there and if it *could* turn into a long-term relationship. *Confusing, isn't it?*

    Because I have met a number of men online over the years, I call myself an *interviewer.* Similar to applying for jobs, you may need to go through a lot of interviews before finding that right one. I refer to my first meet an *interview,* and any get-togethers that follow are considered *dates.*

2. *In Pursuit of the Perfect Partner.* Is there such a thing? I must admit that I am kind of fussy. Even at my age, I want someone to sweep me off my feet with their charm, wit, intelligence, good looks, sexuality, smile, humor, and sincerity. But it's hard to find all that wrapped up into one package. I know that no one is perfect, not even me! If someone has been on these sites for awhile, like me, and are serious about finding someone, maybe your motive is the same as mine, and learning to compromise is imperative.

3. *Long-Term Partner.* This means turning a good relationship into a committed one. Long-term conversations are usually put off while you are determining your compatibility. Different age groups may have different ideas of what the end goal should be. Usually, this is a monogamous relationship, but you both still need to discuss and agree. Live together or live apart?

4. *Marriage.* Many state on their profiles they are looking for marriage. This is a personal choice for some who want the security and the legality of marriage because of religious, family, financial, or whatever reason.

   I don't fit into this category because it is just way too complicated at an older age. People have accumulated assets and have separate families to think about. Co-mingling can be a *sticky wicket.* I have been married and divorced twice and don't wish to go down that road again. I say, "To each their own." I tend to shy away from profiles that state marriage as their goal. It's not my number-one deterrent in sending a message to them, but it might push me one way or another if I am on the fence. Perhaps asking that question to clarify upfront would be appropriate.

5. *Children.* This, obviously, is for people still in their childbearing years and is a valid reason for people looking to have a family, with or without marriage. *This may be a wild guess, but I think most people over 50 do not want to start a family. But them…maybe not!*

6. *Dinner Dates.* Some people *only* want this type of relationship for the company it provides or for a free meal. There are many older people who just want the companionship for a dinner out, as they don't enjoy eating alone and they miss the company. *Personally, I don't like eating out alone.* Dining out is one activity that's most enjoyable with someone else. You

can share the day, news, life, love, the future, or whatever. They don't consider it a *date*, just an evening with a dinner partner. This raises the question: Who pays the bill? Dutch?

Men have told me there are a great many women on dating sites who just want someone to take them out to dinner for free food and/or a social outing. They say that some women suggest dinner on the first meet and expect the man to pay. I don't agree with this because if I had to pay for dinner for every guy I *interviewed*, I would have to come out of retirement to pay my credit card bills! Also, I would rather not agree to a meal so I'm guilt-free when I don't see them again. I always offer to pay my own way on the first *interview*. Dollars would be wasted on people who would only be seen one time.

7. *Part-Time Relationship.* There are several reasons why part-time dating is a motive for many. People, young and old, have so many things going on in their lives today. Many are juggling kids with full-time jobs and have little time for developing relationships. Older people are a lot more active today, with working longer, volunteering, travel, and all the activities available to them. Before retiring, I traveled all over the U.S. for my job, only being home two days a week. I just didn't have the time to cultivate a new relationship.

Most single people over 50 have been married once or twice and have grown children and grandchildren. Many are financially secure and some have been single for a long time. They may not want someone to move into their space on a full-time basis. You might say that most people by the age of 50 are set in their ways in how they do things in their home and with their time. Having someone living with us again would mean that things would be greatly interrupted. It takes a *lot* of compromising, patience, and tolerance to live with someone 24/7. Also, there's the issue of snoring. Let's be honest. When you are used to dead silence, except for the hum of your ceiling fan, how can you expect to get a good night's rest? Overnight is one thing, but every night is quite another.

Having a break from your part-time partner can be a good thing. It gives both of you time to rejuvenate, relax, sleep, and anticipate the next time you are together. I must admit that I fit into this category. However, there's a chance, if I found that *perfect man,* I could be persuaded into co-habitation. Marriage is less likely for me because of its complications at this stage of life, but I've learned to *never* say *never.*

8. *Companionship.* Many older people fit into this category and just simply miss having the companionship of someone to do things with, such as going to movies or enjoying dinner, dancing, and traveling. This may or may not include a sexual relationship. Many men over 50 have expressed to me that many of the women they meet only want a platonic relationship, with no intimacy. The reverse can also be true. Sexual intimacy is not always desired, and often people lose their libido, through no fault of their own, especially in older people or those with certain types of illnesses.

Some people don't have good friends or family close to share their experiences, give them a hug, or just be available as someone who cares. They miss the companionship of someone to talk to or play games with. I have experienced people in my neighborhood whose spouses have passed away or are in a nursing home. After many years of marriage, they are now home alone having to do everything themselves, with no one to talk to. They have a really difficult time adjusting to the loneliness they feel. When walking, I have been called out to come into their home and just talk with them. I worry about people who find themselves in this situation. They do show up on dating sites and are very vulnerable to being taken advantage. Do you know that you can hire a *Professional Companion*?

Many women I know say they want a relationship just for the companionship and nothing more. Most of them have been alone for a long time and say they can't even imagine taking their clothes off in front of someone again. A man probably wouldn't admit that to me, so I won't even ask that question. Negative self-image doesn't go away with age either!

9. *Sugar Daddy/Sugar Momma.* This category includes those *looking* for a *Sugar Daddy/Momma* or who *are* the *Sugar Daddy/Momma*. *Gold Diggers* are included in this category.

Some people want to live a better life than they now have, young or old. Also, many men and women don't plan for retirement. Perhaps their spouse died and left them financially insecure. Therefore, there are definitely people on these sites looking for someone to take care of them in their golden years.

Men and women with *unlimited* funds are included in this category. Many men have lost their spouse, who cooked and cleaned for them their whole married life, while they were earning all the income. They may have a hard time taking over chores and would welcome someone in their life to be their companion and take on those duties.

There are dating sites and apps for every type of situation, including this one.

People looking for a *Sugar Daddy or a Sugar Momma* online are searching for specific things. Widows and widowers are sought after because of the probability of inheritances and vulnerability. It's public knowledge that people watch the obituaries to commit robberies and to prey on the feelings of the bereaved. *Isn't that pathetic?*

Some people search for singles with a beautiful home— preferably one that already employs a housekeeper! Perhaps a yacht moored outside their waterfront home. People searching for their unsuspecting prey may hang out at yacht clubs or fancy restaurants where wealthy people go. Many will go to extremes to find their mark in search of monetary relationships. *Beware!*

Below is a story of a friend's son:

Deceitful Derek
Derek was never too ambitious, and his jobs never paid too much money. He decided that if he became more religious, he would have better luck finding a rich widow—his goal. That didn't work out well, so he decided to sign up on a Christian dating website. According to his family, he really poured on the charm and soon met someone. She had recently lost her husband in a car accident and received a large financial payoff.

In a short time they got married. According to his parents, he has been living quite a charmed life on the farm she owns. He doesn't work, except as the live-in farm hand. The property is now on the market for a handsome sum of money, as they are making plans to move out of state. They've now been married for nine years. Deceitful Derek doesn't spend much time with his family and it seems he's told his bride a lot of things about his past that could be disputed by relatives. Did he have honorable intentions? Time will tell.

Some people only want a companion and travel partner and are willing to pay all expenses like the following person.

Expectations Ed
I communicated with someone online a number of years ago who was in his 80s and said he just wanted a travel companion and would pay all my expenses—no strings attached.

I understand if someone who really wants to travel and doesn't have a partner, they might want to pay the expenses because traveling solo isn't very enjoyable. However, I would hate to have to hide in the bathroom to get away from unwanted advances or to pay my own way home early. Hiring a helicopter to pluck me off a cruise ship could be out of my price range, and jumping overboard can be hazardous to one's health. There probably would be certain unstated expectations, and I didn't want to find out after the ship has sailed. *I couldn't take the chance.*

10. *Sex.* I am sure you are shocked at this one! This purpose is definitely not gender-specific. I know there are women who also get on these sites for the sole purpose of "hooking up."When my son got divorced and set up a profile on an online dating site, he showed me some of the profiles he came across. It was eye-opening for me how many women were only looking for hookups or at least their pictures suggested.

Keep in mind that many of these pictures and profiles are fake. A lot of scammers set up phony profiles with photos of an alluring woman attached, in the hopes of scamming men out of money. Many men and women just want "hookups," but (I think) many aren't real people. To be clear, sex is *not* my end goal!

I have first-hand knowledge of men fitting into this category.

Up-to-Something Frank
I set up an "interview" at Starbucks for coffee with someone I met online who had a noticeable accent, but I found it rather intriguing. After an hour of coffee and conversation, he asked me to go to a popular tourist town, walk around and get something to eat. I finally agreed to go and said I would follow him in my car. Frank was quite indignant that I would want to drive myself, as that was "silly." I resisted for awhile, but he kept making me feel like it didn't make sense to drive two cars. I caved in and agreed to ride in his car, feeling I had not made a very smart decision. Bullying 101!

Up-to-Something Frank parked the car several blocks from the main street in a secluded area. I questioned him about parking off the beaten path, but he scoffed it off. We walked down the main street looking in several shops and finally going into a restaurant for lunch. It was nice, and then he held my hand walking back to the car. Once in the car, Up-to-Something started making his moves. At first it was kissing, and it quickly moved into more. I pushed him off me several times and said that he was moving a bit too fast for my taste. Finally, I raised my voice and told him to "Take me back to my car...NOW!" He mumbled something and then drove me back to my car. Thankfully! We never spoke again.

That was the first and last time I ever made this kind of bad decision when meeting someone on a dating site. I knew better, but I let him bully me into something I knew I shouldn't do. It could have turned out so much worse. You *never* get into someone's car the first time you meet and let them drive you *anywhere. Red flag! Oh, there are more stories to come that fit this category.*

Florida has the reputation of having a 55+ community with one of the highest STD rates per capita in the USA. Older people must not feel they can't contract sexually transmitted diseases at their age and that condoms are no longer required. Someone forgot to tell them that age has no affect on the growth of unwanted microorganisms and bacteria inside a living, breathing body. *Just because there's snow on the mountain and fire in the furnace, bacteria and germs still grow in a Petri dish.*

11. *A Nurse or a Purse.* I always thought the expression was a "nurse *with* a purse." After researching the phrase, it meant either/or. However, the following story contains both interpretations:

> **Two-for-One Terry**
> *I had a neighbor who was in the hospital, where he met a nurse who was extremely helpful to him. They kept that relationship going after he was discharged and resumed his normal life. They had exchanged contact information and, soon after, began dating. They are now building a home together, and wedding plans are in their near future.*
>
> *She has never been married and has no family. My hunch is that this is a nurse (literally) and a purse. I wouldn't think they would be a match, but Two-for-*

One Terry hit the jackpot—he found someone who has the finances *and* who could take care of him if he becomes ill. However, I could be totally wrong. *It's rare, but it does happen<snicker>.*

Now we will talk about the nurse part. It's a real motive for people who do not or cannot take care of themselves medically.

Can't-Afford-Mom Milty
On a blog I read about an American man who went online to find a Russian bride because of his 90-year-old mother, who needed round-the-clock care. Rather than hiring a live-in nurse, this man thought it would be cheaper to find someone to marry who would be able to care for his mother.

When coming to this country, the Russian bride found this man lived in a very remote rural area. It turned out she became his mom's live-in caretaker rather than a bride.

This was a man who found a human solution to his financial dilemma. I wonder how long she stayed or if she was even able to leave. *Risky!*

While researching the "nurse or a purse" category of dating, I had an epiphany! Many articles talk about the older generation (mostly men) being so afraid of getting old and not being able to take care of themselves. This is maybe the reason why many older men want women a lot younger than themselves; they will have someone to take care of them when the time comes. If they were with someone their own age, the odds are that he may end up taking care of her. Now it makes sense why so many men on dating sites are seeking much younger women! *Could it be?*

Perhaps I should change my age requirements to much younger men. I have had many younger-aged men send me messages, and I just blew them off. Maybe this needs further consideration on my part.

Wanting a nurse doesn't necessarily mean just wanting someone for medical purposes. It also could mean someone taking care of the cooking and cleaning, as well as washing clothes and/or performing other household duties—tasks that someone (usually men) can no longer do, have no desire to do, or never did. The over-50 age group is probably more apt to have this motive. I have read online profiles that specifically state these as qualities they are looking for: good cook, enjoys gardening or farm work, etc. You get the connection, right? *After years of making my own meals, it's time to have someone doing this for me and even make my bed!*

Lessons Learned:
- Realize and admit what you are looking for on dating sites. Use the appropriate site(s) for that purpose before you offend, deceive others, or carry on in bad faith. *However, the offenders probably won't be reading this book.*
- Ask the right questions to get at the real reasons why this person is on a dating site.

5. What It Takes to Be a Serious Online Dater

What it takes to be a serious online dater can be summed up in several words: *stick-to-itiveness*—yes, that's a word in the dictionary meaning "dogged perseverance," as well as *patience*, *optimism*, and *determination*.

- *Stick-to-itiveness* to keep looking even when people you send a message don't bother writing back, even if they appear to be your perfect match. The perseverance to keep going, when many of the people who send messages to you look like they have been hibernating all winter in the woods (*I know, beauty is only skin-deep, but some visual appeal is needed to create chemistry*).

  - Perseverance to keep going even after people quit corresponding for no apparent reason.
  - Perseverance to keep coming back after a lot of rejection.
  - Perseverance to send messages even after thinking you may have been scammed.
  - Perseverance to keep messaging others when people 30 years younger than you say they want to get to know you better. *Sure!*
  - Perseverance to keep looking when you want to give up and quit.

- *Patience* to read many, many profiles to determine the ones you want to contact.
  - Patience to actually find someone who could be your match.
  - Patience to sit through some really boring *interviews*.

- *Optimism* is an absolutely required quality to have, especially when you start losing hope that there *is* someone out there looking for you.
  o Being optimistic even when you haven't received a message from anyone in a week or more.
  o Optimism when someone tells you they don't think you are a match.

You need to tell yourself that you are okay with the way you are, because you *are* a person who is deserving of a loving relationship and who is unique and beautiful on the inside and out. You would be a great catch! The words I say to my friends who question my sanity in this pursuit are, "Who knows? He could be the next one I click on."*That's optimism!*

- *Determination* to keep the search going even if that search lasts a very long time. It's strength of will.
  o Even if your best friend found the love of his or her life online the first month.
  o Even if your daughter met her long-time boyfriend after only three online meet-ups.
  o Even if you think you have done everything you can to improve your chances of being noticed.
  o Even if your family and friends say you are crazy to keep looking for someone online.

Maybe, just maybe, the next person you write or talk to will be the person you have been searching for. Perhaps this determination will turn you in a *different* direction to search for a partner.

Determination is going back, time and time again, to review those matches, send a couple messages, and set up another interview—even after you have done this a hundred times. Regardless of the opinions of your friends, who tell you how much better off you are being single without the complications of a partner.

6. Profile Pictures to Impress

Monster Truck
Tiled Floor
Bare and Hairy Chests
Cat, Dog, Horse, and Other Animals
Boats
Work Truck
Fancy Cars
Necks
Groups of People
Kitchen Cupboards
Paintings
Sunsets
Baby Pictures
High School Graduation Pictures
Old Military Pictures
Torso with No Head

These are examples of pictures that actually appear as main photos on people's profiles. *What were they thinking?*

Do you buy a car unseen? Your *main* profile photo is the very *first impression* you make on dating sites. Many people choose to communicate solely on the appeal of that photo. If it doesn't impress them instantly, they won't even read your profile *or* send a message.

On many dating sites, if you are an updated, paying member, you are able to see if someone has actually read your profile. Have they taken the time to find out more about you or is their message solely based on your picture? I was surprised to see that many never went beyond the photo. Therefore, your *main* picture may be the *only* impression of you!

Some dating apps require a picture and simply have you swipe right if interested and left if not. If you don't post any photos, your percentages of getting messages are slim to none. It gives the impression you are hiding something. I see a number of profiles with no pictures at all—not advisable. I've read some of those profiles with no pictures out of curiosity and then requested they add a picture. *No one* has ever responded to that request. *Guess they aren't serious or aren't real.*

Your *main* picture needs to be one of you and only you...not your car, boat, dog, sunset, or your family. Save trophy shots for your photo gallery.

Someone's profile recently had just one picture, a kitchen sink and older cupboards. I wondered why someone would post a photo like this on a dating site. Out of curiosity, I opened the profile and read his bio. He wrote that he had been hacked and his pictures used for scamming. Then, I understood the reason for a kitchen picture (*sort of*). However, how many people will that attract?

Recently, when scrolling through the profile listings, I saw a picture that was blurry and gray. Again, curiosity caused me to click on it to see what it actually was. To my disenchantment, it was a photo of a man in a t-shirt with only a small part of his neck showing. *Yikes! Not impressive.*

On this same online scrolling adventure, I came across a picture that looked like a tile floor. Curiosity again got the best of me, and I discovered it was, indeed, a tile floor! The next picture in his gallery was a business van that had writing all over advertising his tile company. Obviously, this person was using this site for marketing more than dating. *Sorry, I don't go to dating sites for my contractors. Although, I wouldn't mind dating a contractor for the many odd jobs I need done around the house!*

According to a survey taken by Zoosk dating site, 53 percent of men said the first thing they notice about a woman's profile picture is her eyes. After that, 32 percent notice a woman's body, 12 percent her hair, and 3 percent notice a woman's lips. In that same survey, 86 percent of men admitted that they prefer a woman with light and natural makeup over someone with a profile photo who's overdone. There is no mention of men who are drawn to a person's smile. I find that data lacking because the majority of the messages I receive comment on my smile. That's also one feature I specifically look for when I'm searching the dating sites. There's more on this later in the chapter.

Photo Tips:

- Choose your *best* picture as your main one. People base a lot on this first impression of you. If someone is interested, they might check out your other pictures. However, if that main photo doesn't impress them, they will move on to the next person. You may want to ask a friend to help you decide which picture is your best, because this is *crucial*.

- Your picture must be *current,* as in taken in the last six months. This is the *biggest* complaint from people I have spoken to and researched. People post their most handsome and beautiful pictures from yesteryear as their main photo, hoping to attract a message or a click. When someone opens your profile and reviews your gallery, they wonder who is the real you. If all your photos are of your younger days, you are being deceitful and dishonest. Then you go on and describe yourself in your bio as an "honest" person. *That's an oxymoron!* Your goal is to meet someone in person, and...*trust me*...they will discover the truth when this meeting happens.

- *Use captions*, including the date when your pictures were taken. Some profiles I have read commented, "even though my pictures are several years old, I still look the same."*No, you don't!*

  Captions can be a good place to add a little humor. I've seen some very funny captions that caught my attention.

  One profile had a picture of a Labrador dog sitting on a pool table with a man petting the dog. The caption read "I beat her 8 out of 10 games.... Do you want a shot at the title?"

  Another profile had a family picture of 40 people all dressed in white. His caption was "I'm the one in white." Funny!

- A *smile* is likely to be seen as healthy and glowing. You have no idea what a positive impression you make when you are smiling in your photos. Your smile should be natural and genuine. It gives the appearance of being approachable, down to earth, fun, and optimistic. From my online experiences, way too many men's pictures lack smiles. That gives the appearance of being grumpy, unhappy, and that you're not a fun person to be around. That may not be true, but perception is truth.

- *What are you wearing*? Check to make sure your clothing isn't from your high school era, too tight, too baggy, or just not flattering. Socks with sandals? Guys, wear a shirt! I listed these features because I've seen them often. If you are trying to entice someone into your life, wearing that baggy t-shirt and wrinkled shorts just doesn't wet one's appetite. A suit and tie isn't necessary, but casual dress is appropriate. Flowery and bold clothes should also be avoided.

Believe it or not, DatingAdvice.com (Brittany Mayer, 2017) says that potential suitors love it when women wear red and show a *little bit* of cleavage, compared to dressing more conservatively. However, if you reveal too much and post a photo leaning over the counter, what kind of partners do you want to attract? When my son was on a dating site, he showed me some photos that women post. I am not sure their parents would approve. *Unbelievable!* Again, keep in mind that some of these profiles may be fake.

- Don't use pictures that include other people in them, especially your main picture. How will they know which one is you? Is that woman an ex-spouse? You also risk someone in your photo looking more attractive to the reader than you.

If you feel you must post a group picture in your gallery, be sure to add a caption explaining who's in the picture. Remember…people are interested in *you*.

Beware of posting selfie pictures (one you take yourself) because they can be *very unflattering*. The angle the photo is taken may reveal nose hairs or worse. Perhaps you are looking down, showing more chins than you intended. No one should post selfies, especially ones taken in the bathroom. Yes, these appear often because people like to take a selfie using their bathroom mirror reflection. *Not good.*

Very few people can take good selfies, and that includes me! I have tried many, many times, and they all end up getting deleted. They're not complimentary at all.

- If you show photos inside or in front of your car or motorcycle, what is your purpose? People, who are seriously looking for a relationship, want to see and connect with you, not with what you drive. Some may see that Porsche as a status symbol or you being conceited.

- Turn off the camera flash—it can add years to your appearance. Natural, soft light from the sun hides blemishes and aging effects, like wrinkles. By having the flash off, you also avoid flash glare, causing red eye. *You don't want to look like an alien, do you?*

  People who take their best photos during the late night and late afternoon hours get more attention. This could be because photos taken late at night tend to be sexier, and late-afternoon photos are ideally lit when the light is soft, heading into the sunset golden hour, according to Ok Cupid.

- Forget about the glam shots. They will see the "real you" when you meet, and you don't want that first impression to be a disappointment. Candid shots are more likely to receive a message.

- The more photos in your profile, the more your personality is revealed. In my opinion, the magic number is four to twelve. Your pictures need to show you are a fun person doing fun things because that appeals to the majority of people. Photos should reflect your personality, even if serious.

- It's okay to have *one* picture of your lovable pet, but this should not be your main picture. If you're searching for a pet lover, a picture of your pet can strike up a topic of conversation. Zoosk says you should leave your pets out of your pictures, and poses with a dog or cat generate 53 percent *fewer* messages. I personally like the idea that someone I might meet has a love for dogs, as I do. Only one pet photo, if you must.

- Have *at least* one full-body shot in your photo gallery. A potential partner wants to get a good view of your body type. Members with a full-body photo also tend to get more replies to their messages. Men especially base a lot on body type.

- Women posting a sports-related photo in their profile are more likely to get messaged. It's a great way to show off your personality and is a conversation icebreaker. Many men like sports-minded partners.

  A gym picture shows you are health conscious, but multiple gym pictures give the impression that you may be a fanatic. Many men like to show their bodies as a fitness model in the gym, but that can turn someone off who isn't as inclined to be a gym rat. I know of one person who only showed muscle bound arms and body shots with no head showing. *Really?*

- I travel a lot and tend to post pictures having fun around the globe. However, I also post local photos, so men don't get the impression that I travel too often. I don't want them to worry about whether they have the time or financial constraints that would prevent them from traveling, with me. However, I want to let them know that travel is an important part of my life and I'm looking for a travel partner. Balance your pictures, and say something in your bio that would explain potential misconceptions.

  Adding a vacation picture can be a conversation starter and also proves you like to travel, are adventuresome, and like having a fun time. Remember to use a caption.

- I frequently update my pictures and periodically change my main picture, in case that photo wasn't attracting attention. Maybe the next one will.

- The majority of pictures posted are in color. You might want to think about adding several black and whites to give variety and intrigue to your gallery. You will stand out for sure, because most online daters aren't doing this.

Lessons Learned:
- *One* sunset picture is okay, as it can be a conversation starter, but you should *not* use it as your main photo.
- Be careful if every picture shows you drinking. It may give an impression that you have a drinking problem.
- Showing pictures of your children may be better after you have met.
- What can you do if you don't think you're attractive?
  - *Write the best bio possible showing your likes and dislikes, your sensitivity, and positivism.*
  - *Use humor, as the majority of people like humor.*
  - *Remember—beauty is in the eye of the beholder.*
  - *Focus on positive traits that would overcome any outer-beauty issues.*
  - *Can you do something to improve your appearance?*
  - Have someone professionally style your hair.

  I saw a picture of a man who I really thought was an older Daniel Boone, with his raccoon hat and long hair. I clicked on his picture to take a closer look, to find that it wasn't a hat at all but his actual hair. Really, get your hair cut and styled.

  - Women, consider getting some makeup tips and actually following them to enhance your features. Use makeup to cover up unwanted features. Don't forget to keep using these tips when you meet in person.

- If you wouldn't want your children or your parents to see, it shouldn't be posted on your dating profile.
- Have someone else give you feedback on your picture choices before posting them.
- Post a minimum of four pictures.
- Smile in the majority of your pictures.

- Have at least one *recent* full-length picture of yourself.
- Make sure your feature picture is of you alone and shows your best facial expressions.
- Use some humorous captions.
- People are interested in pictures of you.
- Post pictures of you having fun.
- Refrain from posting:
  - Glamour shots
  - Pictures of family, pets, cars, boats
  - Pictures from "yesteryear"
  - Old Army or high school pictures
  - Pictures that are sexual
  - Naked chests – men or women
  - Sideways pictures
  - Pictures that advertise a business
- Post pictures of you in flattering clothes. Baggy and wrinkles don't impress—nor does tight and lumpy.
- Use minimal makeup and display your normal hairstyle (unless it's time for a makeover).
- If you are an artist, posting *one* of your best works to start a conversation is okay, but it shouldn't serve as your main photo.

7. Writing Your Best Profile Biography

Bummer Brent
"Well I'll just be plainspoken. I'm sick of being hurt plain and simple. I'm going through a divorce. So I'm not here looking for love. I've been hurt too much, too many times, by too many women. I won't be a living ATM, or a sex toy, or a trophy boyfriend anymore.

I am not sure what exactly I'm looking for. I do know that I'm done being hurt. I guess for now I'm just looking for friends. Not a casual hookup, or dates or anything like that. I just want to start as friends. But I do want to talk to start moving on. And I'm a fun guy to chat with, so don't be a stranger."

This guy needs therapy and not an online dating site! It's an example of over sharing at its worst and just plain depressing.

Brevity Bill
"I love to take walks on the beach, swim, fish, dance! I collect shells! I make men's jewelry."

Way too short. Not enough to want to learn more about this person.

Political Dog Hater Al
"…If you voted and still support Trump we have nothing in common so get on your Harley and pass me by. Also if you're posing with your dog we're not

> *suitable; I know very well where I will fall in that hierarchy. If I seem a bit jaded, I am. I cannot understand why it should be so difficult; after all I'm attractive, intelligent, financially secure...and modest. Be aware if I reach out to you and you don't answer, you will never hear from me again".*

Keep comments about politics and religion out of your profile. This biography (bio) is way too negative and will lose many good prospects. I'm not sure he knows what "*modest*" means.

Are you impressed with these writings? After your main picture, your bio is the second most important piece of information about you.

On most dating sites, you answer preset questions and then write a brief bio. This is where you have the opportunity to highlight and promote yourself. Write as if it were a sales letter for your dream job. Or dream partner, in this case. Your writing gives a peek into who you are, what you have to offer, and what you are looking for.

Your bio should take a bit of time and thought to create. If you're having trouble, you can find all kinds of tips on the dating site itself, on the internet, and from this book. Take the time and effort to get a "Wow, I really want to meet this person" response. It should be unique, fun, and brief, but *cannot* be done in one or two *sentences*.

Make a list of your top *10* qualities or activities you enjoy and then write a one-sentence story for each. Example: "I love to travel because it gives me the opportunity to learn about different cultures, but I'd like a travel partner to share these experiences," or, "Viewing life with optimism and a positive attitude are two of my best qualities."

Make another list of the top *five* qualities or requirements you are looking for in a partner and write a sentence about each of them. Example: "Cooking together would be great, even if you just like cutting the vegetables or being the taste-tester," or, "Meeting someone that enjoys outdoor activities is important in keeping healthy and enjoying nature. What are your favorites?"

Your profile should say *positive* statements about what kind of person you're looking for, rather than qualities you *don't* want.

No negative statements about people or past experiences. Your goal in your written bio is to make the reader feel curious about knowing more about you. I get totally turned off when I read bios that talk mainly about what they *don't want* in a partner and a relationship. It makes that person sound very angry and makes me wonder if he is a guarded or distrustful person. First impressions are perceived reality.

Most people write their bio on their own. However, it is a great idea to have a friend—an honest and trustworthy one—read it as objectively as possible. Their feedback is really important, to present you in the best light possible. People don't portray themselves positively in the majority of profiles. I can attest to that by hundreds, or probably thousands, of profiles that I've read. *Unbelievable!*

My son reviewed my profile and gave me interesting feedback from a male perspective. Some of the things he wanted me to write seemed awkward and uncomfortable. However, he's been involved in online dating himself, and I thought he must know what he's talking about. *I felt kind of weird having my son help write my dating biography!*

How would these online dating bios rate on a scale of 1-10, 10 being really good? These are all real examples as written:

Breathless Bob
"My hobbies are movies my goal is to find someone that do not play games i am a very romantic person and I definitely do not have time to play I love old school music and jazz."

I would give Breathless Bob a "2." I was out of breath after reading with no punctuation breaks. It's way too short and lacks proper grammar. The only things I know about him is that he likes movies, thinks he's romantic (not sure what he actually means by that), likes jazz and oldies, and he doesn't play games. There's nothing unique, positive, or fun in this bio.

Loss-for-Words Ed
"Xxx"

This is all that was written on this bio. Isn't that eye-catching? I would rate Loss-for-Words Ed a-10. Also, he answered the preset question, "How ambitious are you?" with *"Not Ambitious."* Now I understand.

Below is a two-part question that was included in my online dating survey:

* Who wrote your profile?
    * 73.2 percent created their own
    * 20 percent had someone help them
    * 6.8 percent not applicable (*not sure how that works*)
* If someone gave you feedback on your profile, what advice did they give you?
    * Too restrictive in what I was looking for in a guy
    * Too long

o Be more specific
o Give more detail
o You don't sound like a fun person

Do's

- *Be Positive and Optimistic.* Even though you are angry about some of the people you have dated in the past, refrain from making your profile into what you *don't* want rather than what you *do* want. You must be upbeat and cheerful in your word choices.

- *Truthful.* Honesty is the best policy. That includes your age and your answers to the profile questions. If you smoke, say you smoke. If you drink, say you drink. If you want an honest and trustworthy partner, you must first be one yourself. Dishonesty will show its ugly head sooner or later.

- *Speak about activities* you *currently* enjoy. If you are willing to learn some new activity, state that. For example, do not say you like to kayak but really haven't done so in 20 years, or any other activity, for that matter. If you cannot hike because you have a bad back, don't list it. Don't list playing cards if you don't know what a *suit* means. You get the idea.

The following are examples of what people wrote and what reality is:

Activities Listed in Their Profile	Truths Discovered
Bike riding	*"My bikes have flats, probably rotten."*
Golfer	*"I haven't golfed since college."*
Kayaking	*"I owned a canoe years ago"*

- *Sense of Humor.* Most everyone loves a sense of humor. It doesn't have to be jokes, but brief humorous remarks strategically placed are great. Oftentimes, good humor overrides looks or other negatives someone might have. I have read the same joke about men who compare themselves to an old car many times. It's only funny the first time reading it. The key is to be original, amusing, and flattering all at once.

- *Proofread.* You would not believe how many people omit punctuation and misspell words. Proofread as if you were the person reading it online. Would you be impressed or excited to meet if it was you?

"Honest hard-working romantic man seeks attractive honest dedicated woman to spend time with her dancing shopping picture together get to know a gather and become friends"

This writing lacks punctuation, but is somewhat decipherable. However, it's too short to actually give someone an insight into who he is.

In a study of typos in dating profiles (*Datingsitesreview.com, 2019*) it was found:

> ➢ 75 percent of online dating users were turned off by dating profiles when they notice that they had spelling errors.
> ➢ Only 33.5 percent of participants noticed the errors and called attention to them
> ➢ Simple spelling errors were perceived by respondents as a sign of inattentiveness, while grammatical errors were seen as a sign of lower intelligence. However, both types of errors were linked to lower attraction scores.

Do Not Write About...

- *Medical conditions*—omit those for now. However, be up front with someone fairly early in your communications. Some disclosure should be done sooner rather than later, as shown in this scenario below:

  ### Forgot-to-Warn-Me Leo
  A good friend of mine went golfing for her first date with someone from an online site. After she finished teeing off on a hole, she strolled back to the golf cart and sat down. As she turned to speak to her date, he was holding his prosthetic leg in his hand. Up till that moment she had no idea Forgot-to-Warn-Me Leo had an artificial leg. Needless to say, she was caught off guard, was shocked and speechless. She wished she would have known ahead of time.

- *Your Neediness or Loneliness. Never* say the word "lonely" anywhere in your writing or how much you miss your deceased spouse/partner and want to find someone just like him/her. It's a sure way to turn good prospects away.

- *Fake Poetic Verbiage.* Too many profiles go on and on about the philosophy of love written as love sonnets created by a poet or borrowed from a poet's book from the library. These types of profiles sound like someone else's words and really do not impress most women. Also, scammers use this kind of language to lure vulnerable men and women. A profile needs more information other than love lasting forever and ever. (See Chapter 17: Poets, Philosophers, and BS'ers.)

- *Lengthy.* Long-winded can be boring to the reader, and if you add weirdness to the mix, that gives an impression you may not want.

- *Weird.* OMG! Weird is hardly enough of an adjective to describe some of the people on these sites. If you think someone is weird, beware that he or she can have danger potential beyond their weirdness.

  NOTE: Check out Chapter 22: Just Plain Weird, to read about the dominant/submissive or the guy who shared his masturbation schedule.

- *Negative and Pessimistic...All three below are written verbatim.*

  Shouting Shawn
  "IS THERE ANYBODY OUT THERE WHO REALLY MEANS WHAT THEY SAY???
  Not here to bs anyone..."

  Rules According to Rick
  "Three simple rules:
  1. *If you don't look like your picture...you're buying me drinks until you do.*
  2. *If we're not physically attracted to each other there can be no hope of a romantic relationship.*
  3. *No sex till the 23rd date!!!!!"*

  (NOTE: This was his complete profile biography.)

  No-Biases Blake
  "...I'm open to date ladies who r not over-weight. No obesity. I enjoy dating Caucasian women only. ...I don't brag I'm not noisy..."

The rest of No-Biases Blake's profile was actually okay. He ruined it by adding the judgmental statement in the middle. Keep your bio positive and fun. No tolerance for being a bigot, racist, or judgmental.

Truth-or-Tell Tim

"I'm just an average guy. I am somewhat motivated, I just don't climb mountains and I don't swim oceans. I'm just looking for my last love— someone to be with and someone to spend time with. I'm also hearing impaired I wear hearing aids, I also wear upper and lower parcels and I have no hair on my head. If I might be what your fishing for and your kind of catch then let's hook up. If not then just keep on fishing. Cause as they say there are plenty of fish in the sea."

It's just a wild guess, but I don't think Truth-or-Tell Tim is focusing on his positive attributes but is *trying* to be funny? I don't believe he had anyone reviewing what he wrote before he posted. There's nothing written about him. Hint: Punctuation would be welcome.

Below are three examples of good bios:

Okay Otto

"I am a very active, happy, kind person with a lot of energy. I would rather give than receive. Sometimes it is the simple little things that make the other person feel special. I'm not a couch potato except for cuddling on the couch at the end of a busy day. I would like someone who likes music and dancing, golf, the beach, traveling and getaway weekends and is willing to try new things. Someone who likes affection and holding hands. It would be nice to be friends first and then go from there."

Okay Otto listed seven positive statements about himself in a brief description—short and sweet, and he did address what he's looking for in a partner.

Witty and Positive Paul

"I am 70 and in really good physical, financial and mental shape! I have no baggage due to becoming a successful world class baggage handler in the past! It's how you handle its disposition. I am honest and have a great sense of humor."

"I love reading a great book, spending time with friends, family and traveling. Although I am "officially" retired, I usually have several projects that are underway. I became a writer and finished my first book (non-fiction) four years ago. Now, I'm working on my first novel. I enjoy attempting to cook gourmet meals usually with a glass of wine in hand. I am also a Steelers and Panthers fan.

Love to travel, especially to Carmel CA, Italy, cruises, beaches, and the mountains. Like to take advantage of warm weather destinations during the winter except for Colorado. I am not a great skier, but love being on the slopes and taking the postcard-like scenery in."

Witty and Positive Paul does a great job of describing himself, but forgot to say what he's looking for in a match. He wrote quite creatively in the first paragraph.

Hit-the-Mark Ricky

"My friends tell me I am funny, romantic at heart, sensitive and intelligent. The machismo stereotype you hear about for Hispanics does not apply to me…I strive to do my best at work but I have never allowed myself to be defined by my work. I am easygoing and comfortable in jeans and flip flops or a 3-piece suit. When it comes to relationships, I strongly believe romance will never go out of style.

I am in excellent health and try to keep it that way by staying active and eating right. I am not into the bar scene or a big drinker, but I do enjoy being active, having a good time, and love to laugh.

For relaxation, I enjoy working out (primarily cycling), fine dining, cooking (not just on a grill and preferably together with my mate), concerts, travel, the arts, music, theater and movies, reading a book together and trying new things and seeing new places. I have grown children and love their company when they are here."

I am looking for a woman who is honest, intelligent, interesting, romantic, and with a good sense of humor. She should be open to new things and be adventuresome, be able to laugh at herself and not take herself too seriously."

Everyone is looking for specific things when they read someone's profile. Besides the fact Hit-the-Mark Ricky enjoyed many of the same activities I do, there are some basic elements to his writing. First, the tone is upbeat and positive. There is no negativity in his writing. Secondly, it includes the things he likes to do, as well as what he's looking for in a match. Lastly, there is a little humor when talking about cooking and Hispanics. I personally love someone with a great sense of humor. This bio could be a little shorter but is still effective.

In addition, Hit-the-Mark Ricky has four pictures in his gallery. The main picture is a close-up of his face, and the other three are taken with trees and shrubbery. Two shots are him looking away from the camera, and one is a full-body photo. Two have sunglasses, and two don't. No group pictures and he had a body shot fully clothed. Kudos to him for his photo choices!

My profile has been proofread by friends and family, with changes made often. If something isn't working, change it up. Did you know every time you make a change to your profile, you get moved up the chain on who gets you as a match? *True.* Imagine how many people are on these sites. You have to pay extra to have your website at the top of the Google searches, and this one technique (tweaking your profile) doesn't cost you anything. Make minor changes frequently.

Lessons Learned and Tips:
- Think about your best 10 qualities and write a sentence about each in a positive way. Can't think of 10? Ask an honest friend.
- Talk about the top five *positive* attributes of someone you're looking for in a partner.
- Be positive and upbeat. Does your bio sound negative? If so, change it!
- Have someone you trust give you feedback on your writing before you post.
- Proofread, proofread, and proofread for correct grammar and punctuation.
- Go back and re-read what you have written and make edits often so your profile pops up near the top of the match choices.
- A little creative humor helps. Even though you have read some other funny profiles, don't reuse in yours.
- Do you sound like a fun person? If not, make some changes so you do.

Spend time on your profile so you write *the* best sales presentation possible!

8. What Do Your Messages Say?

Randy Red Lips
"Hello do you love your lipstick on your mans lips too am looking for life partner to love and spoil forever. Am 73 not 58. Am widowed and lonely and so want to meet you."

This was his entire message...an example of what *not* to write. Randy Red Lips has sexual innuendos and an admitted huge difference in the age he posted versus reality. Not sure how you can mistakenly submit an age that is 15 years different from actual. Plus, he's admitted being lonely. Who wants to cultivate a relationship with someone who sounds desperate and maybe depressed? *Sorry, I didn't wear lipstick very often, and now I don't want to wear it at all!*

Lover-Boy Michael:
"Wow, pretty golf and coffee. I might fall in love!! Hi I'm Michael."

Was Lover-Boy saying I was pretty or that golf and coffee are pretty? Do you want to meet me first before falling in love? Appropriate punctuation goes a long way. I responded to Lover-Boy Michael, but he fell into the "Where did they go?" category, even after saying he hoped to meet me.

I decided to send him another message, asking, "Hmmm. Where did you go, Michael?" Still waiting for a response...and really didn't expect one.

Below are examples of good probing messages:

Example 1:
Good morning, John, I really enjoyed reading your profile and, by the way, you have a great smile. You sound like a very positive and active person who enjoys life, and so do I. What kinds of indoor and outdoor activities do you enjoy?

(Or)*What do you like most about living in (Florida)?*
(Or)*You said you like to travel. Where are your favorite destinations? What did you like most about them? What other destinations are you thinking about?*

Example 2:
Happy Friday! Your picture of the sunset is gorgeous! The colors are so vivid. Where was it taken? I think sunsets all over the world each have their unique beauty. What other pictures do you enjoy taking?

Example 3:
Jane, you commented on your love for painting. I just started working with watercolor and acrylics. What are your favorite subjects...landscapes, portraits, etc? Maybe we can get together sometime and you can share some painting tips?

Example 4:
Ken, are you a Badger fan, being from Wisconsin? I was born and raised in Wisconsin. Have you heard of a town called XXX? It's okay if you haven't, because few know of this huge metropolis of 542 people! What encouraged you to move to Florida?

Now that you've spotted someone you want to send a message to, make it meaningful. You are letting that person know you are interested in learning more about them. The words you choose can have a powerful impression on how you are perceived. Your goal is to use words to highlight confidence and avoid the appearance of desperation or neediness. This advice includes what you put on your profile *and* the messages you send.

VIDA Select, a dating site, recommends the following online dating messages, since they get the most responses:

1. Go for laughs: Funny online messages get responses. The key is to actually being funny.
2. Connect on common ground: The theory is, if you make someone feel you are on common ground, they're more likely to respond.
3. Inspire a Craving: Certain words sound delicious, like *chocolate*, *sundaes*, or *cheesecake*. They make people to want to hear more, especially women. Be creative.
4. Ask an open-ended question (one that needs more than a one-word answer) about the other person.
5. Show off your creative side: Example of something to ask: *"If you were stuck in an elevator for an hour with a famous person, who you would want it to be and why?"*

This is what these all have in common:
- Instantly pique curiosity
- Set you apart from the crowd
- Ask a question

The more messages you send out, the more messages you should receive. That's the philosophy behind direct mail advertising. Why not here? It's the law of averages. Also, the more you write, the better you will get at writing, and the more responses you should get.

Overwhelmingly, dating sites and researchers say January is the busiest month and the first Sunday in January is considered *the busiest day* of the year for dating online. *Lack-luster holiday? New Year's resolution?*

Different sources vary on the best day(s) of the week to send messages. Most say that Monday is the worst day and Thursday through Sunday are the best, with many saying Sunday afternoon being the busiest time. Supposedly that is when many people are bored from a lackluster weekend after having little success meeting someone. It's a day of rest so people turn on their computers, looking for companionship. Maybe they want to start out the week having something to look forward to. Maybe they burned the Sunday pot roast and wished there was someone else to do the cooking. Whatever the reason(s), don't forget to check your inbox on Sundays or send a few meaningful messages!

VIDA Select says the best times to send messages are weekday evenings, when people unwind from a long day. NBC news found that bad weather goes hand in hand with increased activity on dating sites.

Something worth talking about are those messages that have *uninvited* sexual under and overtones early in the "get to know you" stage. Even though I don't respond to them, guys keep sending them. Is that a fetish for men over 50?

Recently, I had to deal with this situation. The following were excerpts of our conversations:

Lustful Larry

"It's time for you to ask me some questions," I said because I was the one asking all the probing questions.

His response to my question was **"Sex questions LOL?**

He asked, "Do you kiss on the first date?"

I told him I was playing poker with friends one evening, and his response was "strip poker?" I responded by talking about the weather, telling him I was purposely changing the subject.

His response to that message was "Yes, you sexy cupcake."

Instead of sending me a "good morning" message, he sent a picture of two people rolling around and hugging in bed. Keep in mind I had only been communicating with Lustful Larry for several days.

Larry sent an emoji clip of a monkey on the hood of a car trying to get to a banana sitting on the dash inside the car. I wasn't sure what the purpose of that message was, but I had an idea of what he was insinuating. I didn't respond to that message.

I commented about his friend dying of cancer and how we need to live each day. His response was, "Yes, let's do it while we can. Lol."

I asked him what "it" meant, and he responded with "lol it sex. We may not last a few more months."

Really?

Now, I had to be direct and said, "Tell me why men your age are so obsessed with the topic of sex?"

Lustful Larry responded, "We're afraid we're about done."

I guess I hadn't thought a man would be thinking about that.

"Well, it turns off people who might otherwise be interested. Just sayin'," I replied.

"Ok, cupcake. Guess we have fun in different ways." He referred to this banter as *"teasing."*

He needs to rethink that technique.

I tried to carry on probing and meaningful conversations with Lustful Larry, but they just came back to comments of kissing, hugs, and sex. I'm not opposed to any of these activities, just not this early while getting to know someone. There is a time and place for certain words and actions.

I had visions of meeting and having to fight him off my lips and body. I find that a bit disrespectful, especially when I tried to divert his obsession more than once. He just didn't take the hints, even very direct ones. I didn't respond to his last message. *Moving on.*

Lessons Learned:
- This may seem like silly advice, but check your inbox on dating sites daily. Don't let a message slip by without noticing.
- Proofread!
- Use proper spelling, grammar, and punctuation.
- Refrain from:
  - Going on and on about the details of your day
  - Telling too much about your life, travels, or children
  - Talking about bad past experiences and relationships
  - Sexual innuendos
- Keep your messages:
  - Focused on the recipient and you—in that order
  - Light, positive, and upbeat

- Ask open-ended questions rather than questions that can be answered with one word.
- If you are really interested in someone, don't *answer* a message with one word. Expand on your answer and send a question back to them. You don't want the recipient to have to work hard at getting information from you. One-word answers give that impression, and I see them quite often.
- Don't click on "Flirt," because the message sent says, "Hi there", or something similar. That message gives the impression that you didn't have the time or desire to actually compose something personal to get their attention.
- Tailor your message to each person. Find something in their profile that stood out and ask them about it.

    Examples:
    o He's a golfer. Ask about his favorite course and why.
    o You both enjoy cooking, so ask about his favorite dish to make, or where his favorite dining place is and why.
    o Mention a posted picture of a place where you have also been or one that intrigues you. Mention that you are both northerners, or ask when they moved from up north, etc.
    o Look for something less obvious to comment on to make an added impression.
- Don't make flowery comments ("gorgeous," "beautiful," etc.) about someone's appearance because that doesn't impress most people, and it sounds fake.
- Don't be overly flirtatious, because that can immediately be construed as BS. Rather, give a non-sexual compliment and show interest in their profile.
- If a person tells you their name, use it in your salutation. People like to be addressed in a personal way. It shows you paid attention to their message and that you even noticed their name.

9. Being Considerate

Loss-for-Words and Rude Larry
"Hi there"

This is an automated message sent when you click "Flirt" on POF. Other sites have similar auto responses that are just as blah. On one occasion, when I received this message, I looked at his picture and read his profile. I decided Loss-for-Words Larry wasn't a match and I didn't respond.

Two days later, Rude Larry messaged, "*Rude*"

First of all, this person didn't put any effort into his original message and the rest of his profile just wasn't impressive. Rude Larry chose to respond by name-calling, which is not a good way to react to someone who didn't respond within a timeline of 24 hours. When I started out on these sites, I answered every message, but it just became too time-consuming.

Many people don't respond to my messages. That *did* bother me at first, and I wondered, *what's wrong with me?* However, I've become used to it now, because it's the norm. It's just takes too much time answering *every* message received if I have no interest in pursuing them further. If that's bad, I apologize. However, if someone takes the time to send a very sweet and thoughtful message, I usually will respond with a brief reply. I've received a number of similar replies from people who aren't interested in me. Thanks for that! It feels good to be acknowledged.

Below are some responses that are considerate and appropriate if you just aren't interested:

> *Thank you for the nice message. You have a very interesting profile. However, I feel I am not your match and wish you success.*
> Or
> *Thank you so much for the nice message. However, I don't think that we are a match. Good luck in your search.*
> Or
> *I've just started seeing someone, and I want to see where it goes* (this could be true or not). *Good luck in your search.*

Lessons Learned:
- Refrain from using "Flirt" or other shortcuts rather than sending a personal message.
- If someone doesn't answer your message, move on. DO NOT send negative comments to them.
- If someone has put in the effort to send you a personal and positive message, a short reply would be recommended, even if you aren't interested in pursuing a relationship with them.

The very first dating website I was on was specifically for golfers.

> **Manner-Less Max**
> *I started communicating with Max, and he asked if I wanted to meet him for golf that following weekend. Of course, I said yes.*
>
> *We were emailing back and forth before meeting that day. In one of Manner-Less Max's messages, he told me his height and weight and asked me to*

give him mine. I politely responded, "Don't you know it's not nice to ask a woman those questions? ☺"

He replied, "Okay, what size golf cart should I order?"

I was flabbergasted! His response was not what I expected.

I don't remember what my exact response was, but he wrote back to me that I must be a fat woman if I'm not willing to share my measurements. What a crude man!

Needless to say, I cancelled our golf date and cancelled my membership on that site. I would have hated to waste time golfing with this shallow person lacking of character. I'm writing this with controlled words!

What makes some people so judgmental or jump to unwarranted conclusions about others? Do people feel they can say whatever they want to others, while hiding behind a computer screen, because they won't be outed? *Yes.*

After Manner-Less Max showed his true self, I remember taking a short break from online dating. For awhile, I thought *"Are all men on these sites like this jerk?"*

Lessons Learned:
- Don't allow someone to put you down. People put others down to elevate themselves.
- There are always going to be cruel and manner-less people in the world. Don't become one yourself.
- Like my mother always taught me—if you don't have anything nice to say, don't say anything.

- Don't jump to conclusions about someone. You may be pushing away someone who could be your best friend and partner.

10. People with Physical Disabilities

There are many types of disabilities that people are dealing with while on these dating sites. In this chapter, I only address *physical* disabilities.

> **Unassuming Al**
> *A long time ago, early in my online dating exposure, I met someone from a dating site for the first time at a nice restaurant for dinner. To my surprise, Unassuming Al had a visible disfigurement on his face. He apparently had surgery at some point, during which half of his jaw was removed. Neither of us brought up the topic. I didn't know how to approach it, or if I should even say anything. I thought it was up to him to start that conversation, and it never happened.*
>
> *Unassuming Al was a very charming gentleman, but I didn't feel any connection to him. Maybe it was the elephant in the room—I'm not sure.*

Lessons Learned (Knowing *what I know now*):
- If you meet someone with an apparent medical condition, make it clear that if they want to talk about it, you're willing to listen.
- Don't let any physical disability or disfigurement issues be the elephant in the room. Once it's out in the open, you both should be able to discuss other topics more openly. *I wish I had in the situation above.*

Below is a brief and creative bio on Tinder, written by Lauren, who lost her arm in a moped accident. She uses humor to poke fun at herself.

Brave Lauren
Lauren, 21
Arms Dealer
Hands down the best catch on Tinder
Face 10/10
Body 9/10
Personality 20/10
Arms 1/2

During my research, I came across stories of people with disabilities and the issues they encounter while looking for a partner using online dating sites. I know how difficult it has been for me. I can only imagine the additional challenges a disabled person has endured.

This following story is from Kelly, a pretty woman in her twenties and a writer, who also happens to be deaf. She gave me permission to tell her story.

On-Her-Own-Terms Kelly
In Kelly's online dating bio, she stated that she had slight hearing loss, thus downplaying her deafness. She wanted to be able to control how and when someone found out about her hearing disability. After communicating online with someone for several weeks, they agreed to meet in person. On-Her-Own-Terms Kelly knew her deafness would then be apparent.

Their first meeting went quite well, to her surprise. After they had been dating for awhile, he told her one night that he had a confession to make. He told her that before they met, he had taken note of a conversation in which Kelly talked about a video she had written called, "What not to do when you meet a deaf person." So, before they first met, he found and watched that video, paying attention to her voice and what she had to say. So when they met, he did everything that she recommended in the video. That's why the date went so well.

At first Kelly was upset that he didn't tell her this from the beginning, but then she was impressed he went out of his way to accommodate her and she felt a "rush of love." He impressed her because he remembered her talking about the video, and even took the time and effort to watch it. He was totally aware that she was deaf before they ever met.

They became exclusive, fell in love, and are getting married.

Kelly's story shows that sometimes, if you give someone the benefit of a doubt, they may surprise you.

In my research I came across stories about people in wheelchairs who talked about how people approached them when meeting online. Before even saying "Hello," they would ask if they were able to have sex. People with a physical disability have shared many nightmare stories about the insensitive and inappropriate questions they get. There are even some people who have an excessive or irrational devotion to disabled people. The receiver of this type of attention gets the feeling of being dehumanized.

The majority of people with disabilities who share their stories online felt people with any kind of disability need to be upfront in their profiles. Some even show full-length pictures of them in their wheelchairs. This will help weed out those who are close-minded. Many talk about their disability jokingly in their bios.

Some physically disabled people say they've been left at restaurants or other venues, with no help to get home and no phone call to make sure they got home safely from their disgruntled date. Where is the humanity in people?

Many disabled people have stories of people who agree to go on a date, only to find out they were just curious. Some of these stories would break your heart, but there are also many successes, similar to Kelly's.

Occasionally, disabled people use humor and like it when their date feels comfortable enough to get in on the jokes. A person who is confined to a wheelchair shared a story about when he went out for dinner with a girlfriend, who blurted out, *"If you don't stop, I'm going to push you down the stairs again!"* in front of a bunch of people. Spectators were shocked, but the couple just laughed about it for days.

What came up over and over from these stories is that the best response is to be treated like a *non*-disabled person—like an equal. If you haven't dated a disabled person, I ask, why not?

Lessons Learned for the *Non*-Disabled:
- Be sensitive to people with a disability and don't ask insensitive questions.
- Examine your biases and prejudices.
- Get to know them more before making judgments.
- Share some of your vulnerabilities before bringing up their disability.
- It can be helpful to say that you would like to know more about this aspect of their life when they're ready to talk about it.

- If they're open about their disability, help them feel more comfortable by listening and joining in on the conversation. However, don't ask insensitive questions. Be respectful.
- If they are joking about their disability, join in without being rude.
- Be open-minded about the possibilities.

Lessons Learned for the Disabled:
- Depending upon your physical disability, it is considerate to share briefly about it in your online profile, or at least in early conversations, so your date isn't blindsided when you meet.
- Focus on all your positive attributes. Don't make your whole conversation about your disability.
- Be upfront from the beginning and talk about how you have adjusted in a positive way.
- If you are able to joke about your issues, that will put the other person at ease. Get them laughing with you.
- Have a positive attitude. If your date doesn't turn out to be a love connection, you may have found a good friend.

11. Scams and Cons

Phishing is a term to describe a malicious individual or group of individuals who scam users. They do so by sending emails or creating web pages that are designed to collect an individual's online bank, credit card, or other login information

A *catfish* is someone who creates a false online identity. *Catfishing* is common on social networking and online dating sites. Sometimes a catfish's sole purpose is to engage in a fantasy. Often, the catfish's intent is to defraud a victim, seek revenge or commit identity theft.

Many mature men and women often feel undesirable at their age and feel they may never find love again. When a good-looking man or woman starts paying attention to them, they feel special, desired, and wanted. Online scammers know this and prey on those fears. They tell you what you want to hear.

> *"These kinds of romance scams are very targeted social engineering attacks, effectively 'hacking' the victim's emotions, rather than trying to perform a technical assault."*
>
> —Nathan Wenzler, *Love& Money*,
> February 13, 2019

People are convinced by strangers online to fork over money and, in many cases, lots of it. Typically, a victim meets someone online, and soon they claim they need money for an emergency, a sickness, legal problem, car repair, or an airline ticket, so they can meet you face-to-face. Don't count on it.

According to Market Watch (Aug 24, 2019):

- Romance-related scams are now the costliest form of online fraud, the Federal Trade Commission (FTC) warns.
- The number of romance scams reported to the FTC increased to more than 21,000 in 2018, up from 8,500 in 2015.
- People targeted by these scams reported a median loss of $2,600, according to the FTC. Losses are even higher for older age groups, with people 70 and over reporting the biggest median loss at $10,000. (On talk shows, guests have reported losses over $100,000)
- Losses from dating-related fraud quadrupled in recent years, from $33 million lost in 2015 to $143 million lost in 2018.
- A company that screens profiles for dating companies says that 500,000 of 3.5 million, or one out of seven profiles, it scans every month, are fraudulent

Around 1 in 10 online profiles is fake, with romance scams collecting nearly $50 million per year in total, according to Online Profile Pros (onlineprofilepros.com).

These figures are alarming. Online daters must be cautious! I've been scammed four times on different dating sites that I know of and have had exposure to many other suspicious dating site members. Because of all the data breaches happening, more and more personal data is available for attackers to use.

Wenzler also states that since these scammers are "*armed with these personal details, it becomes much easier to have conversations that may interest the victim, build trust and ultimately pose a request for money that appeals to some aspect of their personal life that the attacker has discerned from their cache of the victim's information.*"

Bali Guy

I started receiving messages from a man with western-type pictures showing him hugging his horse and wearing a cowboy hat. According to him, he was currently out of the country working in Bali, Indonesia. He wrote a lot of complimentary comments about how nice-looking I was. "Any man would be honored to be with you," he told me, along with many other flattering statements.

He immediately gave me his personal email address and began writing very long messages. I thought they were too flowery and way too long, but I kept responding with short messages. I even had a friend read his first messages, and she, too, was smitten with his writing abilities.

After several days of corresponding, his emails started sounding very possessive. He said things like, "I want you all to myself, you and only you," and, "I don't want you with anyone else because you are all mine."

I was suspicious early on, but now it was just plain creepy and scary. This is the point where I stopped corresponding. Something else that bothered me from the beginning was the fact that his words just didn't match his cowboy-looking pictures. Also, if he loved his horse(s) so much, why didn't he ever mention them in any of his messages? *Red flag!*

Online dating scammers steal someone else's pictures and profile, unbeknownst to them. These people are also victims in these scams. It's not personal; scamming is a job for them. Most of these scammers live in poor countries, such as Nigeria, where jobs that pay well are scarce. They learn that a few hours a day communicating with women (or men) in the U.S. can make them a fortune. *Lucky us!*

Most scammers don't talk to you in person, but if you actually do speak to one, they may speak with a British accent, because it's romantic to most American women. Scammers know this and use it to their advantage to hook their targets.

Men and women have appeared on T.V. talk shows telling their tales of the money they have lost because of online dating scams. Older people are usually the targets, because they have high incidence of loneliness and vulnerability. People have a hard time admitting they have been duped by someone and that this ideal person doesn't really exist. It's very sad to hear how their life savings have been drained or how they have lost their homes because of a love scam. Watch some of Dr. Phil's old episodes to see more heartbreaking stories.

These scammers are very good at reeling you into their web of deceit. If you're not careful, they may use *your* money one day to visit America, the land of opportunity!

Scammer Lessons Learned:
- Be aware that scammers do exist.
- Take things slowly when talking to someone online.
- Ask tricky questions to see how they answer, or if they answer your questions at all.
- It's okay to say "no" and to be skeptical and cautious.
- Don't let yourself be bullied into doing something you know is not right, such as sending money to a stranger.
- Search the internet for any information on this person. If they don't show up, they aren't real. You can also search an email address to uncover online scammers by using sites like Spokeo.com (mixed reviews) and others. There

is a fee for this service, and always check reviews before using any online services.

- Be careful when writing your profile and sending messages to make sure you aren't giving out information about yourself that can be used as bait for a scammer. Don't mention your income, where you work, or your address. Lonely or needy-sounding profiles attract scammers.
- *NEVER send money!* The moment money is requested, stop communicating and report them.

Another kind of scammer is very real and *wants* to meet you in person with the goal of eventually stripping you of your assets— a *con artist*. These people are a bit harder to detect because they have the opportunity to romance you in person. Their goal is to use those skills to win you over. Be aware!

Too-Easy Tim

A friend told me this story about her friend who met a man online.

The female in this relationship had just recently lost a long-time friend and she really wanted a man in her life. The man she met online told her a story of moving a lot, getting rid of all his possessions, and replacing them with second-hand furnishings upon moving to his current rental home. All he had to his name was a television, tools, and a 2015 Honda.

Can anyone detect money issues?

Too-Easy Tim and the woman "consummated" their relationship within the first week of meeting. She told her friend that she was "in love."

Geez, my nails grow slower than that!

Two months later, they were talking marriage.

Wow! This man was on a mission and moving at supersonic speed to get there! She married Too-Easy Tim within three months of meeting him and was hiring a lawyer six months later, fighting for her bank account.

Con Artist Lessons Learned:
- Check if any of the *Red Flags* listed below apply to your situation.
- Be cautious if someone is pressuring or bullying you into moving faster than you think is normal or comfortable for you. If friends are skeptical of this person and tell you to slow down, it would be wise to listen.
- You or someone you know should do a background check on the individual. It may be money well spent. At minimum, search this person on the internet for any additional information, positive or negative.
- If you are asked for money, even for little things, start to question their motives.
- At a minimum, wait six months to a year before jumping into a legal relationship. This would give you a better idea of what this person is all about and what their motives might be. If they really care about you, they will slow down the pressure at your request. If not, it's a *red flag.*
- If you think marriage or even living together is what you want to do, get legal advice from a lawyer. A prenuptial agreement would be a good idea.

There is a true story on Netflix about an online dating scam that would be *very* beneficial to watch. It's called *Dirty John* and is very eye-opening on how con artists operate!

Red Flags

- ➢ The first thing you notice is improper English and sentence structure because most scammers aren't English-speaking.
- ➢ The majority of scammers want your personal email address or phone number so they "can more easily communicate" usually by the first or second message. This is because they only have a temporary profile and want to get off the dating site as soon as possible.
- ➢ Scammers spend hours communicating with you daily, grooming you to feel a real connection with them. They tell you all the words and loving phrases they predict you haven't heard for a long time, all the things a long-time lover would say to you. They are counting on you soaking up the attention like a very dry sponge, so you're hooked on their *endearing* love for you. They profess their love forever and say that you are the only one for them. The only difference is that you've never met them and probably never spoken to them personally. Ask yourself— *is this reality?*
- ➢ Most scammers say they're out of town working or visiting and will be back soon. You can't meet them in person because then you will know immediately they aren't who they say they are. In one of my case studies in the next chapter, Houston Guy wasn't too bright because he gave out the name of the company where he said he worked. I traced it and found what I needed to know. So can you.
- ➢ You ask them simple questions they rarely answer, such as what activities they enjoy. They just keep on writing about how much they care for you and how you can have a wonderful life together
- ➢ Fraudulent profiles usually describe themselves with philosophies of love and tell you how adored you would

be. They go on and on about how they will take care of you. *Wouldn't we all like to have that after years of taking care of ourselves?*

➢ Scammers usually pretend to be widowers and will know from your profile that you, too, are a widow. They will use this vulnerability to get you to trust them, knowing it will be easy for you to bond with someone who has also experienced a loss. Women love romance, and scammers know this has been missing in your life. They will steal poems off the internet to make your heart melt.

➢ All the scammers I've encountered have asked me how long I've been on the dating site. This is important information for them because they think the longer someone's been on a dating site, the more desperate or vulnerable they *might* be.

➢ Most scammers will use terms of endearment almost immediately in their communications. Popular names and phrases include, "Baby," "Hey, beautiful," "Gorgeous," "I love you, baby," "You are the most beautiful woman—how have you stayed single so long?" as well as, "I can't wait to see you," and, "I want you all to myself."*Double-red flag!*

➢ If you see their pictures, and they really don't seem to match the words they write, go with your intuition. If something doesn't make sense or appears odd, be aware.

➢ If you ask for more pictures, he probably won't send any. If he does, they will probably be family photos, but he won't be in them, especially if he has used some else's picture for his profile.

➢ They might tell you about a huge business deal they're about to close, and once done, they'll come see you. They just need a little more money to finish the deal, or they'll lose everything. He might say that family members have invested as well, but the bank won't be able to give him/her the last bit they need. They might lose the deal

and all the money their family has invested. Now you start feeling sorry for them. Don't fall for it!
➤ Scammers will eventually ask for money to help them get back home and for other strange reasons. They never got to that point with me, but if I had let things move forward, it would have only been a matter of time.
➤ They could have a family emergency, or someone needs a life-saving surgery, but they can't afford it.
➤ They could be having problems with their passport or visa and need money to solve the problem so they can get to you faster or at all.

By this time, you are in love with him, and you don't want to see him or his family suffer. You want to help, and you end up wiring the money they need. You may never hear from them again, or they may keep finding reasons for you to keep helping them until you're out of money.

And then there's the opposite side of the coin: fake or stolen pictures of beautiful women attached to profiles full of sexual innuendo—or flat out asking for sex—and later asking for money or credit card information.

Beware and be informed! Be smart!

Action Plan

Below is an Action Plan by Lisa Copeland, author and dating coach for women over 50. It's to help protect yourself from a scammer and keeping your online dating journey safe and your finances intact (*Is dating after 50 different from when you were younger?*" *(April 29, 2017 – dated but pertinent)*:

1. Date people who are local.
2. Keep emails short and sweet.

3. Spend no more than a couple of hours on one or two phone calls, max.
4. Meet this person within two to three weeks.
5. If someone tells you they'll be out of the country for a month or two, tell then to give you a call when they get back.
6. Upload their profile picture to Google Images. You'll be able to see if the image matches who he says he is, or if the picture was stolen from someone else.

Ms. Copeland also hosts the weekly radio show called *You Can Find Love After 50* on Going Solo Network Radio and is a guest writer on www.HuffPost.com.

If you believe you've been the victim of a dating scam, you can report it to the FTC online using its complaint form. They suggest including the website where they met the scammer in the complaint. You should also report scams to the dating site.

Some websites with more information:
https://www.consumer.ftc.gov
https://www.moneycrashers.com
https://www.aarp.org/Datingscams
https://www.romancescams.org
https://www.truthfinder.com
https://www.scamwatch.gov.au

12. Scammer Case Studies

Ironically, while I was in the middle of writing this book, I received a message from someone online named Eric who said he lived in a city about 40 minutes away. He was my age and had nice pictures, one with a cute dog. We conversed back and forth all day. The following is a verbatim account of our conversation, which turned out to be a scam. This is a perfect example how to spot the red flags from a real online scam conversation. My red flag comments are in bold throughout this encounter.

> **Scotland Guy** (written verbatim)
> *"Hi, there. I am Eric. I really will love to get to know you better here if you don't mind you got a very beautiful smile, where did you get that lovely smile from?"*
> **Improper punctuation, but not unlike many other messages at this point.**
>
> *"Good morning, Eric. I got my smile and love for life from my mom, for sure. Totally agree—love for life and new places! Sad to hear of your loss. How long have you been a widower?"* (Stated in profile)
>
> *Eric replied, "Thank you for taking the time to reply me on here...well I lost my wife 5 years ago thing has never been the same since she passed away...well you seems real nice and I hope we can talk More and see how it goes between us Sandy what do you think?"*
> **"reply me" is improper structure. All scammers I have encountered say they are a widower and state how much they miss their spouse.**

"Sounds good to me☺", I said.

"So tell me how long have you been on this site and what's your experience?" asked Eric.
Almost every scammer has asked me this question. I believe they are seeking out people who are becoming disappointed because of being on a dating site a long time with little success. That may make someone more vulnerable.

"Too long!" I responded. "I've met a few people, dated a little, but also have been scammed, too! It's not an ideal way to meet someone, but I keep optimistic. I know many success stories. I do have a lot to offer the right person because I enjoy life and being active. How about you?"

"Sandy I think we are perfect for each other and also share same goals in life if you don't mind I would love to have your phone number possibly if you have WhatsApp messenger we can talk more on there what do you think?"
How does he know already that we are perfect for each other? Scammers always want you to stop communicating through the dating site and use texting or personal emails. This was the first request to use WhatsApp. This site offers free text and phone calls anywhere in the world.

"Sure. I have WhatsApp, too. It's great when you travel out of the country! I would love to talk more about the things you enjoy."(I sent my phone number.)
Now I'm getting very suspicious but decided to play along to see where this goes.

"Smiles that's just perfect...I'll text you in a bit on WhatsApp ok?" replied Eric.

"Ok," I responded.

"So I guess you wouldn't be talking to another man on here since we now share contact with each other is that correct Sandy?"
Wow! This request usually comes later, but Eric asked quickly to only talk to him. They don't want anyone else occupying your time or attention.

"Let's see how things go, Eric," I responded.

Now jumping to the texts on WhatsApp:

"Hey Sandy how are you its Eric from POF"
(He also included his picture from Plenty of Fish (POF) like maybe I forgot who he was?)

"Hi, Eric! Keeping warm?" I asked.

"Smiles. Can I have a picture of you if you don't mind Sandy?"

"Are you going to throw darts at it? ☺"
I sent a picture from my POF profile, although I knew he could have gotten the same picture from my profile.

"Wine tasting," he said.
Where did this statement come from?

"Where is the 669 area code? You mean you aren't a native Floridian!!??" I asked.

I noticed his phone number, and it definitely wasn't an area code from Florida—where he said he was from.

"Well I didn't get my cell phone from Florida Sandy"
"Wow you look really beautiful I must say"
Constant flattering remarks are really common in these types of online encounters and he's deflecting.

"Thanks, you aren't so bad yourself! So—where did you live before coming to Florida?" I asked.
Keep asking probing questions.

"I love your glasses Sandy"
Nothing special about my glasses, but again, another flattering remark and still not answering my questions.

"Well I use to live in Little Rock Arkansas"

"What about you Sandy?"

"I moved here from Minnesota. Brrr! Sure glad I'm not there now! Is that your cell area code?" I replied.
I keep asking the same question, trying to get an answer.

"From Arkansas"

"No, that area code is from CA," I replied.
(Of course, I checked, and it's the area code for San Jose, California.)

"I bought my cell phone when I went to a press conference meeting in CA"
People don't normally live in one place and buy their cell phone in another.

"I hope that doesn't bother you Sandy."

"I have been to Minnesota a couple of times I am sure its lively there beautiful weather out there."
If he's been to Minnesota, why would he say he's sure it's "lively there?" Poor sentence structure is common with scammers because they are usually from another country, like Nigeria.

"So tell me how long have you been divorced now?" Eric asked.
Added "now "at the end of sentence...unusual.

And also do you have any kids?" added Eric.

"A little strange to have a cell phone number from a state you didn't live in," I commented.
He didn't respond to my comment. I wanted to see how he would react, because I already know he's a scammer.

"Been divorced 17 years. 2 kids and 4 grandkids. U have any kids?" I asked.

"No my late wife didn't have me any kids before she passed away."
Note the odd sentence structure—"have me any"

"I'm a little curious about your last message to me on POF about my not talking to others," I said.

"☹☹☹," Eric sent.

"Oh I'm sorry about that. To be honest with you I don't like talking to multiple people Sandy that's just me I'm sorry if it bothers you."

He asked me not to talk to others and be exclusive. Scammers tend to be possessive. They want your undivided attention on them.

"I am a man with great sense of humor, God fearing and very accommodating."
In my experience, "God-fearing" isn't a common way to express spirituality in a dating conversation in the U.S. Accommodating?

"I am very sincere and honest person, am caring, kind, social, smart, intelligent, passionate, friendly, romantic, and I believe in the truth and honest of love. **(Yeah, right!)** *I am really a very sincere person when it comes to sharing feelings and emotions with that special person and I am really am down to honest about things I say and do cause I don't like hurting people's feelings, cause everyone has a chance to laugh, so why do I make them sad….."*
Very strange structure and run-on sentences, not like American English.

"Ok. Let's talk about the activities u enjoy the most," I asked, changing the subject.

"Well, I enjoy almost everything sandy," Eric responded.

"Well, my hobbies are swimming, fishing, going for walk in the park and lot more. I'm very adventurous. More also I like traveling as it's also the nature of my work"
"More also" is strange wording.

"What about you sandy tell me more"
In my previous scam experiences, the scammer wouldn't answer my questions. Eric was a more responsive scammer, which tells me scammers are

getting a little smarter on how they communicate. They normally cut and paste the same nonsensical and lengthy love philosophies.

"I enjoy all kinds of outdoor activities and of course traveling. What's the nature of your work?" I asked.
Get them to answer this question in order to gain more hints of a potential scam that you can research.

"I'm an electrician. I am an Electrical Contractor. I am into Underground Cable Installation of the high-voltage direct current (HVDC) electric power transmission system. my work station is located at the outskirt of North Scotland we are trying to transfer electrical supply to an undeveloped part of North Scotland. Sub-Sea power link, capable of carrying up to 1200 megawatt (MW) of electricity moving electrical transmission to an undeveloped part of North Scotland, hope you don't mind we stay connected?"
First of all, he is now telling me he is working out of the country. *Big red flag!* Second, who would give that much detail regarding what they do? No one that is for real.

"How do you propose developing a relationship when you are traveling to Scotland?" I questioned.

"Sandy I believe if one needs to be happy you don't need to consider the distance as long as you keep the connection and communication going on that's just fine a relationship can happen."
They always tell you that distance is not a problem, even when you know it is. If you are first intrigued by someone, you may give them the benefit of a doubt, even though you may be skeptical. At this point I'm sure he is a scammer, but wanted to see what more he was going to say.

"Are you busy sandy?"
He's getting nervous because I hadn't responded to him for a couple hours.

I replied "Yes, doing some volunteer work today."

"Wow, that's really lovely of you"
"Lovely of you" isn't a common American expression.

"Well, life just isn't about me, right"? I responded.

"Guess so. It's about helping those in need as well."
Again, he is answering and engaging like a normal person, where many scammers don't. However, keep in mind that they are grooming you.

"Exactly," I replied.

"So sandy I hope you don't mind about the distance. I have the strong belief that we are connected together for a reason"
Connected together for a reason? What reason could that be? They usually will profess this type of connection as being *divine* or *meant to be*. They are trying to suck you into believing in a spiritual relationship or fate—even from afar and having never met or spoken to you in person.

"Talk later," I said.

"Ok then please text me when you can alright? Take good care of yourself"

I replied, "That almost sounds like a goodbye? I just have to get some bookwork done."

"Smile. Why did you say it sounded like a good bye sandy?"

"The words "take good care of yourself" "sounded a little like a goodbye. We just met (sort of), so really didn't think so☺," I responded.

"Well I didn't mean it the way you are saying it sandy. Believe me we just met and we are having a good conversation and I must tell you it's worth it. I asked you a question and you still haven't answered it"

"What question?" I asked.

"I was asking if you have issues with the distance sandy."

"How often are you out of town? You gone now?" I said.
I'm trying to get back to the "out of town" issue. They are ALWAYS out of town or out of the country. That way you cannot meet them in person. It also sets up a situation later when they eventually will ask you for money to get home or for some other reason. Keep in mind that the money questions don't come up until they think they have you sucked into their romantic clutches. They never got that far with me, however.

"I'm currently in Scotland," answered Eric.

"For how long?" I asked.

"And I will be in town in three months time"
So now he will have three months to groom his mark without their questioning his existence or being able to meet. A scammer will keep pushing that timeline further out because they have no intentions of ever meeting you.

"Do you have family in Florida?" I asked.

"Well I'm the only child of my parents," Eric responded. "Just cousin but he moved to Germany with his family early this year"

Of course he doesn't because they don't want you to have any way of researching them. It does set up my next question, though.

"So, who takes care of your dog?"
He posted a picture with a dog on his profile.

"My housekeeper," Eric answered.
It's unrealistic that a single average man who is gone for three months at a time would have a housekeeper or even a dog. Scammers typically have animals in their pictures, giving off a warm and cuddly feeling about them.

Now I'm ready to call him out…

"Eric, I have been on these sites for awhile, and you remember my telling you about experiencing several scams? I know all the red flags, and you, my friend, are a classic example of an online dating scammer. Do yourself a favor and get a 'real' job and stop preying on others!" I stated as my final response.

Surprise! No further communications were received, and his messages and profile disappeared.

Not-So-Smart Houston Guy
A very nice-looking man (they are always good-looking and age-appropriate) started sending me messages about how nice-looking I am and how he wants to get to know me better. His profile sounded great, but scammer profiles

94

all do. He started sending long messages and didn't answer normal questions that I asked. He was also out of town working in Houston, but would be back to the area in a week or two. As we talked, it was always another week or two.

He answered questions about his work and told me the name of the company where he worked. Because of his sharing this information, I thought maybe he was for real. I also had a friend read his first messages to get her opinion if he sounded real or not, because I felt unsure after the second message. Her opinion was he was just a talented writer and thought it was sweet. This is what they count on.

When he kept writing more and more gushy, lovey-dovey messages, I became more suspicious. I decided to do some research on the company he said he worked for in Houston. When I entered the name online, it did pop up. However, just beneath the company link was another link titled, "Scam," and below that was a very familiar statement…a phrase from one of Houston Guy's emails that I recognized.

I clicked on the scam link to find word-for-word writings matching his emails to me. There was a different name at the top and bottom, but the exact word-for-word verbiage. Upon reading further, it was revealed to be a Nigerian scam that had been reported by many victims. What they do is copy and paste their corny words of endearment over and over to thousands of online daters. I was right to be suspicious and to investigate.

I sent him one last message that read "SCAMMER!!!" in very large letters.

No response, of course.

Coffee Bean Guy

I started chatting with a man who lived locally (so he said) but had to travel to South America because he was a wholesale coffee bean distributor. It sounded a bit far-fetched, but I kept the conversation going to give him the benefit of a doubt. We tend to rationalize things that sound a little off when we're motivated. The conversations from him weren't the normal poetic, beauty-infused accolades that other scammers often use.

I asked him a number of questions about his business and why he had to personally go to South America. He kept answering my questions, but those answers started sounding so unbelievable. For instance, he had to personally find the farmers and check out the quality of their coffee beans? Then he had to set up all the shipping details in person. This didn't sound like the job description of a part-time distributor from a small town in Florida.

He was a total scammer!

13. They're Hot and Then They're Not

Hot-to-Trot Hal

Hal's profile indicated we had a lot of things in common. His pictures were very attractive and had the look of a person I wanted to get to know better.

He called me "Baby" very early in our communications, but I wasn't put off by it. He was six years younger than me, and I liked that. Hal was still working and traveled around the Tampa Bay area for his job. One day he called me and said he was only several blocks away from where I lived. I panicked! I asked him, "How do you know where I live?" He said I had told him, and I emphatically insisted that I hadn't.

Hot-to-Trot Hal wanted to come over, but I told him I'd rather get together across the street at a restaurant. He said he would meet me in the parking lot because he was still on the clock and couldn't stay long. After hanging up, I quickly checked our past texts and, I'm sad to say, I did tell him the housing development where I lived. Still, his showing up that close to my home made my suspicious heart skip a beat because we've only spoken on the phone up till now. I slipped into my shoes and drove across the street to meet him in the parking lot, as he suggested.

Hot-to-Trot Hal looked just like his pictures, and I liked what I saw. We talked for a brief time and then exchanged some very long kisses. We had talked about our kissing skills in earlier conversations, and now we were just checking out the skills we both professed to have. He passed! We definitely had a spark between us.

A week later, after talking daily, he called and said he would like to stop by my house on his way to a job site. I hesitated for a moment and then reluctantly agreed. He stopped by and stayed for about an hour. Hot-to-Trot Hal did have wandering-hands syndrome, and I had to put the brakes on his hormones. It just seemed to me he was testing the boundaries and didn't seem upset when he learned what they were. In spite of that, it seemed like we were heading in a good direction.

After that, Hot-to-Trot would set up times to meet and then cancel at the last minute because he had to go out of town for a job, but I understood his work commitment. We kept talking and texting, but Hot-o-Trot Hal still didn't ask me out on a "real" date. First, his daughter-in-law was pregnant, and he needed to watch his grandson. Then the daughter-in-law went into the hospital and delivered a baby boy and he needed to take his grandson again when she got home. Then his new grandson developed jaundice. There seemed to be a lot of reasons why we couldn't meet up again.

Several weeks passed, and still no mention of us actually going out on a date. I had already decided that he couldn't come to my house again unless we went out on an actual date. I did tell him that I wasn't interested in a "hookup," as I wanted to make sure that his intentions were in line with mine. Of course, he whole-heartedly agreed.

It just didn't appear Hot-to-Trot Hal was making any effort to see me. I made the decision to move on and didn't send any more messages. It's my philosophy that if there's a will, there's a way. If Hot-to-Trot Hal wanted to see me, he would have. From the lips of a male friend, "For men, it's all about the chase." Perhaps he thought the chase was over. Although he didn't get the pot of gold!

Weeks later he did send a "Merry Christmas" message, and I returned the greeting. We've had no conversations since. Perhaps he was hiding the fact that he was married.

Hot-to-Trot Hal surprised me by not continuing a relationship that he seemed genuinely interested in cultivating. Perhaps he had good reasons why we couldn't get together, but when they started feeling like *excuses,* I had to evaluate our situation and move on. In this case, if Hot-to-Trot was sincere in his explanations and was truly attracted to me, he would have continued pursuing me and proven my assumptions wrong.

Hot-to-Trot probably sent out a lot of probing messages to multiple people and just found someone more interesting. That's okay, because I admit, if I don't find messages interesting, or if they avoid answering my questions, I will stop communicating. In this case, however, we had met twice, and sparks were flying.

We would like to think that we're extremely interesting and desirable, but, sometimes it doesn't work out. What this experience showed me is sparks still do ignite, and that's what I'll still keep searching for in a relationship.

Lessons Learned:
- Don't give out any indication of where you live to a new dating prospect, even if they ask. Once you get to know and trust them, re-evaluate giving them that information.
- If someone wants to come to your house *before* you've been out together on a real date in a public setting, you should question his or her motives. Meeting them one time doesn't constitute *knowing* them. Trust is earned.
- Once someone has shown interest by taking you out on several dates, and you feel safe with them, *you* can invite them over, but never rush. If you feel uncomfortable or you are being pressured, delay until you're ready.
- Pet names like "baby" early in the relationship might be offensive to you. If it is, address it with the person right away. If not, enjoy it.
- If you make an effort to keep a relationship going, and it's not reciprocated in a timely fashion, back off and see what they do. If he or she doesn't pursue any contact, a relationship with you is probably not important enough for them. If this happens, just move on.
- It's hard not to feel rejected, but don't beat yourself up over a lost relationship that was flawed from the beginning. You are worthy of someone who will treat you with respect and provide the relationship you are seeking. It's as the old expression goes: *"You have to kiss a lot of frogs, before finding a prince."*
- Evaluate your messages to make sure they are positive, upbeat, and not all about yourself. (Refer to Chapter 8: What Do Your Messages Say?)

14. Just Too Needy

Clutchin Greg
Greg told me he was in a previous relationship with someone who ended it because she wasn't interested in holding hands. I thought that sounded strange. After three dates, I understood why.

The first "interview" was just for lunch. The second was a dinner date at his house, where he cooked me a nice steak dinner (he seemed harmless). On the third date he took me to a concert. Clutchin Greg grabbed my hand immediately after getting out of the car and held it all the way into the venue. It got to be a bit much when he kept holding my hand while I was trying to take off my jacket. Clutchin wanted to hold my hand throughout the entire concert, and he had a hard time letting go, even when I got up to use the restroom. It was difficult to even clap for the performer. OMG! It was like a leach had taken hold and I couldn't shake it loose.

Again, when I tried to put my jacket on after the concert, I had to tug his hand loose. What a turnoff! When Clutchin Greg drove me home, I told him that we just had our last date.

Holding hands is a really nice thing to do when you care about someone, but having someone hold your hand without letting go is an immediate forced intimacy. It's as if they just don't want you to get away. Clingy, clutchy and too much!

Lessons Learned:
- If someone is making you feel uncomfortable by forcing too much touching, express the fact that you are uncomfortable with what they are doing.
- If someone continues after the discussion, they are not being respectful to you, and it's time to move on.

Below is a story about staying with someone longer than I should have. I rationalized that I could make it work when it just didn't fit. It was the winter I rented a house in a highly sought-after golf community with two other women to see if I liked the area. I set up an *interview* with a man I had been talking to online and who lived nearby.

Way-Too-Needy Norm
Norm greeted me with a flower when we met. "How sweet," I said. His clothes were a bit large for his body, but he was a nice gentleman. While we had something to drink, he started telling me about the death of his wife just four months prior. I figured that was the reason for his weight loss and clothes not fitting. I asked Norm if he was still grieving his loss. He was adamant that he was ready to move on and have someone in his life. I thought four months was a bit soon, but believed what he was saying.

Soon, Way-Too-Needy wanted a new couch that was long enough and wide enough for us to cuddle together and watch TV. I thought that was a bit premature on his part, and that's when I started feeling a little discomfort that he was moving a little fast.

We talked a lot, and he was agreeable to anything I suggested. He even let me take him shopping for new clothes that actually fit him.

Way-Too-Needy lived in a nice golf course community, but he didn't golf. He wanted me to teach him how to play and even bought new golf clubs right away, but really didn't enjoy the game. I think he just wanted to please me. I didn't pressure him in any way, but he still wanted me to go golfing. Once, when I passed his house in the fairway, I saw him out amongst the trees, taking all kinds of pictures of me. That was cute, but a bit strange at the same time.

When I was sending texts to a friend one day, he looked over my shoulder to read what I was writing. I mentioned to him that was not appropriate. Soon after, I was on my computer reading emails and again, he was standing over my shoulder trying to read. I reminded him that was private, and it's not his right to be invading my space in that way. One day he went into my purse looking for my car keys.

Whoa! Invasion of a woman's purse! That was a complete intrusion, and I insisted he never does that again unless I tell him it's okay first. I believe his 49-year marriage created his pattern for "no privacy" behavior. Not appropriate.

Speaking of privacy issues, Way-Too-Needy Norm had removed the door to his master bathroom and thought that should be totally okay with his partner.

Not this partner!

> *"It's no big deal, because couples should have nothing to hide from each other" was Way-Too-Needy Norm's response when I expressed my dislike of the missing door. Guess I'll just use the guest bathroom, when necessary. Later, Way-Too-Needy asked that I not use the guest bathroom because it takes more water when flushing.*

OMG! You have to be kidding. Frugality is okay up to a point. I kept using the guest bathroom whenever I felt like it.

> *Way-Too-Needy wanted to show me all his financial and banking information, which I really did not think was my business. He kept saying "That's what couples do—share everything." I surely wasn't going to show him mine!*

> *I'd already had one back surgery, and then my back went out again one day while I was teaching him how to play pickle ball. It was only six weeks into our relationship. I was in a lot of pain and had a hard time even walking. Norm insisted that I stay with him so he could help take care of me until I got better. That is when the neediness really ramped up. He was his wife's caretaker, because she had years of severe back problems.*

See any similarities here? This is the moment when I made a bad decision and took him up on his offer, because suddenly I had become needy.

> *Way-Too-Needy Norm wanted to do everything for me. His persistence in giving me massages was constant. He kept insisting that he drive me to physical therapy until one day I had to tell him flatly "no." I was capable of driving that short distance*

myself. I felt suffocated and finally had to sit him down and tell him that he was smothering me. He said he was sorry and would work on that.

Several times I brought up that he hadn't completed his grieving process yet. He didn't like my saying this at all. I asked him questions about his life with his wife, and I listened to his stories. It sounded like they had a very happy life together. Again, and again, he assured me that this is what his wife wanted him to do—move on right away. In my heart I knew it wasn't true and that it was too soon. He was still in caretaker mode.

At that time, I was spending every summer at my lake property in Minnesota to get away from the Florida heat. It was nearing the time for me to make the drive north. Way-Too-Needy Norm announced he wanted to make the drive with me so he could help me with the driving because of my back. Also, he really wanted to see Minnesota and check out the great fishing on my chain of lakes.

I assumed he would drive up with me, spend a couple weeks, and then fly back. Oh, no! That's not what he had in mind at all. He wanted to spend the entire summer with me in my '44' RV, even though I told him that it would be very tight quarters for that long of a time. Panic set in, but I didn't have the heart to tell him he couldn't come after he had told all his friends how excited he was to finally fish in Minnesota. He researched the lakes I lived on, all the fishing opportunities, and how he could spend quality time with me. He was so excited, but I knew it wasn't going to last.

What a coward I was! For someone so confident and assertive, I cannot believe that I allowed this to happen. Keep in mind that the 27-hour drive would have been a very painful experience for me with my back, and he was willing to help. *So now who's the needy one?*

> *He was in Minnesota with me just one week, and I was pulling my hair out. My good friends confronted me about what they saw in our relationship, and it wasn't positive.*
>
> I kicked myself for letting him come with me, knowing it wasn't going to work out. Now I have to gently get out of my predicament.
>
> *Way-Too-Needy had gone shopping right away to purchase a new tackle box and all kinds of artificial bait and gear. When I saw these purchases, I knew I had to tell him my true feelings about our living arrangement. Before he opened all the tackle packages he had just purchased, I broke the news that it wasn't going to work and that I wanted him to fly back to Florida. He was shocked, sad and then very angry. Way-Too-Needy Norm flew back home ten days later.*

That was the longest two weeks of my life. I understood his feelings, but felt relieved when he had departed. I let this relationship go on far longer than it should have because of my own neediness at that time and my reluctance to hurt someone's feelings.

Ironically, within a month of his returning to Florida, Way-Too-Needy Norm met another person with back problems and got engaged within several weeks. Are you seeing a pattern? He actually sent me pictures of his new fiancé and her new shiny engagement ring. Did he think I would be jealous? Happy for him and *me*!

Lessons Learned:
- Evaluate why you are putting up with characteristics or situations that you really don't like or want.
- Trust those feelings of being uncomfortable and communicate those feelings more strongly early on.
- If unwanted behavior continues, be committed to your expectations and end the relationship.
- Don't let *your* issues dictate bad decisions.
- Express your true feelings with sensitivity, even though it may hurt the other person.
- If you are trying to fit a round peg in a square hole to make a relationship work, stop, because it won't. Don't let a relationship go on longer than it should when you know it will not last. It's unfair to them and you.

15. Where Did They Go?

One day you get messages from people who seem very interested and then…poof, they are gone. Surprising possibilities revealed.

Edwin the Ghost
Edwin lived in Clearwater but said he had been taking care of family business in Puerto Rico the past four months. He said he was heading back to Florida in a day or two, where he lived near his family. Edwin the Ghost asked if I would go out for dinner and dancing when he got back. He also wanted to set up a date for kayaking. Yeah! He's excited about the same things I enjoy.

"I'll give you a call when I get back as soon as I can so we can get together for dinner," he said.

That call never came.

Tight-Lips Jack
Jack and I communicated seven or eight times while I asked short questions, trying to get more information about the activities he enjoyed. All of his responses were very brief with no elaboration or questions back for me.

Tight-Lips said he liked to kayak. I responded by saying that I hadn't been kayaking since my maiden voyage the past spring and would love to. I then asked, "Do you like to bike ride?"

He answered, "I haven't done that for a long time."

I replied, "Tell me more about the things you enjoy doing. Golf? Just want to see what we have in common." No response.

I noticed his pictures were gone from his profile. I wrote back "Why are your photos now hidden?" No response.

If someone's entire profile and pictures suddenly disappear, it's a very good chance it was a scam in the making or they found someone else and hid their profile. Another reason for no further response is that he didn't think we were a fit. If that were the case, a message ending our conversations would have been the considerate thing to do. No one likes dealing with ghosts, and unanswered questions lead to insecurity—*mine*!

Many of my relationships online would start out sounding promising as we messaged back and forth. Sometimes we would move to personal emails or texts. There would be multiple messages per day over a period of several days or a week. They would seem very excited about learning more about me and *appear* to be really engaged. They would talk about future activities together and then...poof, no more messages. I would look back and rehash what I said, trying to find some clue why everything came to an abrupt halt.

Many people online send out a lot of messages just to see who will respond. As quickly as they message, they disappear. This is a reality of online dating.

Surfer Paul
Paul and I were corresponding back and forth for awhile, until he just stopped. I went back through our conversations to see what I may have written

that would be the cause. I had just asked him, "What do you like to do on rainy days?"

He answered "indoor surf on pof (Plenty of Fish), lol!!!!!"

My response was, "Ha-Ha! That gets tiring! Today I'm getting ingredients ready to make chicken broccoli wild rice soup tomorrow. Serving Tuesday night at a little gathering and time is tough tomorrow if golf is on (I golf Monday mornings). In fact, I'm heading to grocery store right now. I'm checking on my disabled neighbor on way because his wife is out of town."

After not hearing a response, I reread my message and realized I went on and on about nothing of interest to him. I beat myself up pretty good about what I wrote. Maybe it was the reason he didn't write back or maybe not, but w*hat was I thinking?*

Most online dating sites give their members a chance to send a "flirt," make someone a "favorite," or send the message: "I want to meet you." I usually respond with a short message and make a comment about something they said in their profile or about a picture. Perhaps I will ask them a question…something to start a conversation. Sometimes I say I'm responding to their "flirt" or to the fact that they added me as a "favorite," so they know *they* had initiated the contact. That's where it often ends. It's perplexing why they bothered contacting me in the first place.

Then I heard about *bots*. I did some research and found interesting information concerning what a number of dating and chat room sites do to get business. It was a sigh of relief to find out that it wasn't anything I may have said or anything to do with me at all.

When online, we believe we're connecting with a real person. In reality, bots drive more than 60 percent of web traffic according to Talkspace.com. Programmers hired by the site design chat bots to simulate real conversations long enough to convince you to buy something or give you the perception there is a lot of traffic on that site, so you'll join.

They're programmed to pick up on keywords people write in their profiles and use those words to get conversations started. On dating sites, they want you to believe there is a lot of activity happening so that you continue with that site or consider upgrading for a fee. If you get a lot of responses, you're more apt to pay more money.

Most online dating bots take the persona of someone physically attractive. They primarily target users by being flirtatious or attempting to lure them with the prospect of naked photos and videos. These types of requests have not been my experiences to date, but bots are a very real phenomena on dating sites.

As the founder of Zones, Nikolay Pokrovsky has spent many hours dealing with bots, and talks about the bot strategies on dating websites and messengers. He said many chat bots will communicate long enough to offer users a link that leads to malware or a porn site that uses bots for marketing. CNET (2020) proclaims that Plenty of Fish (POF) is filled with bots and scams.

There are some clues that this *person* could be a bot. For instance, try to outsmart it by asking questions one wouldn't typically ask in certain situations. A human may have to think for a minute, but would be able to answer. A bot would inadvertently reveal itself or stop corresponding.

In the same article mentioned above, Chris Orris, a self-described "computer geek" suggested some questions that may reveal a bot:

> "I hear music in the background or is that just me?"
> "You know, you sound a lot like my mother (or ex-wife)."
> "You sound like you're having the same kind of Monday I'm having."
> "I saw something like what you're talking about when I was visiting Spain. Have you ever been to Spain?"

Orris said the key is focusing on the "person" you are talking to. Because this person doesn't exist, the bot will have trouble keeping its character believable and consistent.

Most bots are not very good at responding to *onomatopoeia*—here's the definition according to Webster: *the naming of a thing or action by a vocal imitation of a sound associated with it, such as buzz, cuckoo, sizzle, hmmm, or hiss.* See what responses you get using these sound words. Bots tend to use generic responses like "Tell me more," or, "Let's talk more about that." Try using some *onomatopoeia* words or phrases. *I just learned a new word!*

Sarcasm is a huge challenge for bots. They will interpret sarcasm as genuine and won't be able to answer a joke. Try using some sarcastic jokes. Here's one to try: "Take my advice—I'm not using it."

Keep in mind that if you are on Integra, Facebook Messenger, or other social chat platforms, you face the same type of bot invasions. *Beware.*

Now that I've learned about the presence of bots, the disappearing phenomenon is not as baffling to me as it once was.

Below are other reasons why some people just stop communicating:

> ➢ Found someone more interesting.
> ➢ They were married and their wife found their profile on a singles dating site. He's now missing fingers, preventing him from using a keyboard.
> ➢ Reconnected with a past friend.
> ➢ A potential scammer felt bad about targeting me because I appeared to be too kindhearted. *I wouldn't bet on this one!*

I prefer to think they were *all* bots! I'll never know for sure. Whatever the reason, I'm not going to beat myself up because a conversation ended as quickly as it started. However, I'm a very honest person, who usually says what I mean and mean what I say. I expect everyone to be the same, but they're not! I do know that we don't deserve to be treated that way. There is a chapter in this book that addresses how to be considerate when dating online (See Chapter 9). Not much we can do about bots, except to weed then out early.

Lessons Learned:
- Early in your communications, try using some onomatopoeia words and phrases to help determine if you are talking to a real person or a bot.
- Refrain from going on and on about the details of your day.
- Avoid telling too much about your life, travels, or children.
- Focus your messages on the recipient first and then you.
- Keep your messages light and positive.
- Move on.

16. Not Ready Yet

Stuck-in-Time Rob

Rob's profile sounded like a great match for me; he even had a beautiful dog for a companion. He had been a widower for over one and a half years after a long and loving marriage, as he described it. Rob was ready to find a new loving relationship.

Our first "interview" was for coffee, and it lasted for three hours! We were both on a coffee-high and able to converse so easily. The conversation just flowed from one topic to another with ease. He showed me a picture of his beautiful standard poodle that was his wife's service dog and now was his faithful companion. Of course, I pulled out Niko's pictures, too (my adorable Havanese).

We decided to meet for a second time and take our dogs on a walk along the causeway. It was obvious that both of us loved our dogs and the outdoors. Lovely idea! I was very interested in learning more about Rob and introducing my Niko to his poodle to see if they hit it off.

The day started with lunch at a local bistro right on the causeway trail. It was a warm and sunny day—perfect for getting to know each other better. The dogs got along famously while we walked the entire length of the trail and back. It was a very pleasant day, and I could already tell that I was very interested in this man and it appeared to be mutual.

Stuck-in-Time Rob told me he was going out of town in a week to spend time with relatives in a northern state, but we still texted every day after the dog walk. Then, I didn't hear from him for several days, until I received the following text:

"It's taken a few days to respond to you because I not only wanted to take things slow but also I needed to find the right words. Our conversations and times together were great but made me realize that I am thinking too much of my wife, and I'm just not ready. I know with your personality that you will find someone, but right now it's not me. If you would like to reach out when you get back from Colorado, maybe I'll be in a different mental state. Thank you for being who you are."

I was totally surprised but appreciated what Stuck-in-Time Rob wrote. A few months later, I did send him a picture of Niko's first kayak ride, just to keep me in his thoughts. I texted him again when I got back from Colorado as he requested. However, I didn't get any response. I have no way of knowing if his reasons were true, but at least he sent a very thoughtful text.

My experiences in this category have only been with widowers, but certainly could occur with anyone just getting out of a recent relationship. Widowers can make very good partners because they are more likely to be committed, having been in a long-term relationship that ended through no choice of their own. However, I've had several situations like this and now am a bit cautious with widowers of less than a couple years because two's company, three's a crowd.

Lessons Learned:
- Watch for more signs of someone not over a previous relationship.
  - teary eyes when talking about the previous relationship
  - inability to make any plans
- Ask questions that get them talking about their previous relationship so you can assess their responses. "How long has it been?" and, "Are you seriously ready to start dating again?"
- Look for pictures still hanging in their home of their deceased spouse or past partner. If they won't take them down, there's your red flag.
- Stuck-in-Time Rob was an example of someone who didn't realize he wasn't ready until after two dates. What they say and what they actually feel may be two different things.

17. Poets, Philosophers, and BS'ers (Bull Shiters)

Shakespeare's Apprentice Ken—written verbatim
(Try only taking a breath when there's a period.)

"Good Morning I Love Ur Beautiful SMILE and I hope we can Build a Solid Foundation of Friendship TOGETHER u HAVE a Smile that could Brighten the Very Darkest of Rooms as U entered It I live in Lakeland as well a big plus is someone who has a great Sense OF HUMOR and I hope we can Build a Solid Foundation of Friendship TOGETHER U WANT TO MEET FOR COFFEE SOON OK OR EXCHANGE phone NUMBERS together and text and send pics TOGETHER ok. I'm OLD FASHION ROMANTIC AT HEART KINDA MAN THAT KNOWS THE TRUE MEANING OF BEING A GENTLEMAN THAT KNOWS HOW TO TREAT A LADY LIKE A LADY SHOULD TRULY be TREATED take a chance on Me ok I NEVER EVER WANT U WALKING BEHIND ME NEVER EVER BUT WALK BESIDE ME WHERE SHE BELONGS AS MY EQUAL PARTNERS WALKING HAND IN HAND to PLUS to BE ABLE TO look OVER INTO MY LADIES HEAVENLY EYES AND JUST SMILE AT EACH OTHER AS WE WALK OFF INTO THE SUNSETS TOGETHER THROUGHOUT ALL ENDURING TIME."

Whew…I'm out of breath! I think he's trying to tell me he's romantic and would treat me like an equal. It also tells me that he may or may not have a high school education because of his writing skills. Do you feel like he's shouting with all those capital letters? The lack of punctuation makes it *very* difficult to read. I'm pretty sure he didn't proofread his message before sending, or perhaps English is not his native tongue.

Philosophers and poets primarily talk about their philosophy of love, life, and togetherness. The BS'ers use words they think will impress you, but instead make you feel skeptical of their motives and identity. After all, how do they know you are the most beautiful person in the world? They haven't met you yet or even communicated with you. I could be physically beautiful, but be an ugly person inside wearing a fake smile. *There are a lot of beautiful people on the inside, but the cover is a little worn.*

One time I felt annoyed and answered a message similar to this and asked him how he knew I was a "beautiful person." I went on to talk about inner and outer beauty. Not surprisingly, I didn't get any response.

Ken, the Bologny Guy
"I am a kind, caring, compassionate man who desires to find that special someone with whom I may create a great love story. I am well educated, articulate, dependable, and I love to laugh. My desire is to love a caring lady with all the passion, dedication, faithfulness, and intention possible.

Is that it? What activities do you enjoy? What are you looking for besides a "caring lady?"

Full-of-Crap Thomas
His first message to me was "Hi there."

I responded, "Hi, Thomas. You wrote a lot of nice things in your profile, but I would like to know about the things you like to do."

"Thanks for responding to my short message. It's been a great deal for me to see such a beauty like you here. I liked your profile very much. You sounded sweet and it was nice reading it. When I joined this place, I never expected to meet a woman of your type because you sooo adorable and beautiful. For how long have you been on this site?" he replied.

There are a few red flags in his message. First "such a beauty like you" is a bit flowery. Second, he asked me, "For how long have you been on this site," a common question scammers ask when targeting those they believe to be lonely women or men. Also, starting a question with "For" is unusual. Full-of-Crap Thomas didn't answer my question about activities he enjoys, either.

Lessons Learned:
- Proofread your messages.
- Don't use capital letters unless it's the first letter in a sentence or a proper noun.
- Use punctuation so the recipient doesn't have to figure out what you're trying to say.
- Refrain from using all those flowery words that can be construed as fake. It's okay to write about their smile and their looks, but don't go overboard.
- Potential matches mostly want to hear about you and what you like to do rather than philosophizing about life and love.

- Reread the messages you compose. Put yourself in a recipient's place and ask yourself the question: Would *you* want to know more about you based on what you wrote?
- Beware of potential scammers when someone uses flowery, poetic, or *bologny* talk.

18. All About Him

Fancy Pants Brad

I received a notification that someone had made me a "favorite." This piqued my interest, and I clicked on his profile. He was an avid golfer, liked to travel, showed a picture of a cute roadster, and seemed like an interesting man. He was a little older than my normal matches, but I decided to check him out anyway. I sent him a message, and he quickly responded.

That same day we started talking on the phone. He said when he originally tried to message me through the dating site, he received a message saying he wasn't able to because he didn't fit my parameters. Not to be deterred, he made me a favorite, and that is how Brad got around the dating site block. I gave him kudos for his tenacity.

Our first phone conversation sounded like Brad could be a really good prospect. He was a golfer, had a sense of humor, and was financially sound because he owned four cars, which included his "everyday" Tesla, '66 Corvette, a Porsche, and, of course, that cute roadster I saw on his profile.

Fancy Pants told me about his past girlfriend, whom he had met on the same dating site and what a wonderful relationship they had before she passed away from cancer the year before. Their first date was on a golf course, and he wondered if

I could be the "next Brenda." That felt a little strange to hear, but I guess I understood, sort of. The culmination of that first phone was him asking for a golf date in two days and if I would make the tee time.

First date, and I'm making the arrangements?

When we met at the golf course, he was better looking than his pictures and in good physical shape for his age. He said he usually walks 18 holes of golf twice a week. I was impressed, but I'm not able to do that, so we took a cart. He's a really good golfer and was a gracious cart mate.

I've always said that you can tell a lot about a person when you golf together. *So I thought.*

During our golf game he made a comment about oral sex out of the blue. I pretended not to hear it and didn't respond. He asked me if I got what he said and I replied that I did and dropped it. Aside from that, we had a great day of golfing and he treated for a bite to eat afterwards.

Two days later we went out for dinner—again, he asked me to make the reservation. After dinner, Fancy Pants asked if he could come over to my house to meet Niko, my furry, four-legged friend. I thought I knew him well enough to consider it a safe request.

I gave him a tour of my home, starting with my painting room. I'm an artist so I showed him the cabinet of my hand-painted glassware and the canvas paintings decorating my walls. His only comment was, "Oh," and then he walked away.

I guess I was waiting for some "oohs" and "aahs," or some questions or comments, but I got nothing. After all, who wouldn't think my talent is the best they ever saw! That was my first real clue that maybe things were just about him.

That evening he shared with me that he hid his profile on the dating site because he thought he had found his "second Brenda."

I responded, "Wow! Took down your profile...already? Also, my name is Sandy, not Brenda!"

He also told me, "You won't have to ever pay for anything, being with me," and he talked about a trip to Biloxi he was already starting to plan, where we would golf and gamble. That did sound fun—and I wouldn't even have to plan or pay for it? No one had ever said I "wouldn't have to pay for anything." I did tell him I felt a little uncomfortable with that arrangement, and I would want to pay sometimes. He said my home-cooking would be enough payment for him, and I let the subject drop. Fancy Pants Brad didn't want to travel internationally but really wanted to travel the USA. That sounded okay to me!

It's been difficult finding someone at this age who is in good physical shape, loves to golf, appreciates home cooking, likes to travel, who has the financial means to enjoy life, and who wants to treat me to all those life adventures. Why wouldn't I be interested in this man, in spite of a couple red flags, right?

The following weekend I invited him to dinner, but Fancy Pants Brad wanted to go to brunch and a baseball game with his friends instead. However, after the ball game, he still wanted to come over for that steak dinner I had promised.

All during the baseball game, he was buried in his cell phone sending and receiving messages. Again, the words "oral sex" came up out of the blue, and again I ignored the comment.

What was up with him and this topic? It just turned me off.

After that evening, I decided that oral sex being brought up twice really made me feel uncomfortable. Therefore, I sent him a message and said, "I've been wrestling with our relationship of less than two weeks and have decided that we aren't a match after all. If you must know, the last comment about oral sex was the clincher for me. This topic is too early in our relationship to be brought up. It's something you work up to, and you brought it up the first time we met! For future reference, any classy woman would feel the same way. I'm looking for a nice guy who respects me in that way. Good luck to you, Brad."

He quickly responded with, "I'm sorry and I apologize to you, have a great trip." In a couple days I was leaving on a two-week trip out of the country.

Shortly after I left on my vacation, I started receiving text messages from Fancy Pants asking about my trip. Then he said he "missed me talking his ear off." We texted about trip stuff, and then he said how much he missed me and asked, "Will you forgive me please? Whatever it takes."

I asked Fancy Pants, "I am curious, though, why you brought up oral sex the first day we met."

He stated, "I don't think I did the first day. I'm sorry, my mistake. I can make up for it, but only if you want me to. Don't give up on me."

I decided to give him another chance, thinking maybe I was being too picky. After all, our conversations were mostly very positive, and he seemed genuinely sorry.

After I was back from my trip, Fancy Pants Brad asked me out for dinner. During the meal, he was on his cell phone checking messages and taking calls from his ex-wife, which I found very inconsiderate. Often, he interrupted me with news about baseball game scores or was telling me about some of his text messages. These constant interruptions were really becoming annoying, especially when he didn't get back to what I was talking about before his interjections (red flag).

What's wrong with this guy? Wasn't he ever taught manners growing up? Well, there weren't cell phones at the dinner table when we were growing up!

The next day during a phone conversation, he asked, "What day are you having me over for another meal?" He certainly was bold, but I thought that was just his assertive personality. I fussed over making a nice meal, making appetizers and a blueberry cheesecake because he really liked desserts. It was fun, because I missed cooking for someone. Plus, it was an excuse for me to have cheesecake!

When Fancy Pants Brad arrived, he immediately stretched out in the recliner and commanded, "Turn the TV to the news." I replied "P-l-e-a-s-e turn on the news?" A bit bossy, I thought.

When appetizers were served, he made no move to extract himself from his comfortable position. I had to bring the appetizers within his reach. Now I felt like a maid in my own home. He then told me "Your TV is crap. I can't get the baseball game." What a slam!

I replied with "Excuse me?" I turned off the news while we ate without asking permission. Oh, yes, he did extract himself from the recliner to come to the table to feast.

Now the red flags were flying all around me.

At least a half dozen times while I was talking during dinner, he would interrupt me again with baseball scores. He avoided talking about my trip and actually made some negative comments about my traveling. I was thinking how rude he was, and it must be time for him to leave, but didn't say anything. I was avoiding a confrontation, not knowing how he would react.

Several times during our walk after dinner, neighbors would stop and chat with me and fuss over Niko. Fancy Pants Brad wouldn't say a word and just kept on walking. He didn't seem to care about talking to anyone or being friendly in any way. I'm a very social person and certainly would want my partner to be friendly to others. Red flag.

He commented, "I was going to drive my Porsche tonight, but thought that would be too much for your neighbors to handle."

What a shallow thing to say. I rolled my eyes so far back that my head hurt!

Fancy Pants wanted to watch a movie, but scolded me for not being able to use the clicker good enough or fast enough to find one. I told him he was being too bossy and to please stop it.

By this time, I wasn't feeling warm and fuzzy towards this home intruder and just wanted to watch a movie and have him leave. *In reality, it should have been the other way around.*

During the movie, he was asking me to plan the weekend activities. Whatever I wanted was fine with him. I played along and suggested golfing on that Saturday. He answered by saying he wanted to go to dinner Saturday night and golf Sunday.

So much for "whatever I wanted."

As the movie ended, he told me he was tired and wanted to know if I was going to invite him to stay the night. I was startled and then laughed and said, "No." That's when he got out of the recliner and started walking toward the door without a word. I asked where he was going and he said he was going home. I said, "Wow, that's abrupt." But I was glad. So I went to the refrigerator and tossed him a bag of leftover ham from dinner that I had promised. He said to let him know when I had made tee times for Sunday, but it "had to be in the morning." Then he was in his Tesla and gone as I watched from the doorway. Adios!

I was right the first time about this guy, but he talked his way back in my door.

The next day I received a text saying, "Don't make the time for golf Sunday, I'm committed to working a car show."

Perfect, I thought! He made this easy for me.

I replied, "Ok, and something came up Saturday. I'll have to pass on dinner, too."

His response was, "Okay fine"

Needless to say, I moved on, because I'm *not* the next "Brenda!" I had mentioned earlier that I was writing a book. To show how into himself Fancy Pants Brad really was, he asked if my *whole* book was going to be about him. I replied, "No, just one chapter" and here it is.

If you grew up being told to be nice and not to hurt people's feelings, you may let negative relationships go on too long rather than telling your partner early you don't like how they treat you. I have a pattern of letting personal relationships fade away rather than face the person and the conflict head-on. However, when you know a relationship isn't going in a positive direction—and you *do* know—dig deep to overcome that feeling of wanting to avoid the conversation. We need to tell them at the very point when they are mistreating us or acting selfish.

I don't like getting into a potentially heated argument, especially when I'm in a place alone with someone I don't know that well. You can't judge how someone will take bad news. Walking away may be the safer thing to do.

Fancy Pants Brad still texts me every couple weeks, wondering what I'm doing and inviting me to play golf with him. At first I replied like a friend would, but we really aren't friends. Finally, I sent him a reply that I should have sent right after we parted ways. This is what I sent, and I didn't expect a response:

> "Brad, to be honest, in the four times we were together, it was very evident to me that a relationship with you would be all about you. I want someone who wants a 50/50 relationship. Someone who doesn't want to be my boss. I'm telling you this as constructive feedback for you to think about. Good luck to you, Brad."

He never reacted to my final message but occasionally still sends a message asking about my dog or asking how I'm doing. I don't respond because that ship has sailed.

Lessons Learned:
- It's okay to give second chances, but as soon as you see the red flags, address them. Depending upon the responses, make your decision to stay or go.
- When you see someone on their phone constantly when they are with you, ask them politely to turn it off when you are together.
- If you're feeling that you wish they would leave, tell him or her to leave.
- Keep safety in mind when choosing where and when to deliver bad news.

- If your intuition tells you this person is just all about him, this won't change, so move on.

19. No Money for Playtime

Can't-Play Curt
Curt and I met for coffee for our first "interview." He was a very nice man, and our conversation went well—until I asked him about his thoughts on traveling now that he was retired. He said that he hasn't done much traveling but sure would like to. Curt asked what places I have traveled to in the past. After I told him about of my travel history, he acted sheepishly and said, "I really am not able to keep up with you with all the traveling you have done and probably want to do in the future."

I quickly replied, "I'm really good at finding good deals online and actually travel very reasonably. Traveling internationally wouldn't be an absolute requirement, but having a travel partner to visit places in the U.S. would be great."

Softly, Can't-Play Curt responded, "I just couldn't afford your lifestyle."

Keep in mind that I had travel noted in my profile as an activity I enjoyed and wanted a partner to enjoy with me. He must have missed that part.

I usually seek out people who say they enjoy traveling in their profiles, assuming they are financially able to travel if they respond. I have found that not to be true in a lot of cases, such as Curt's. Some may not confess their lack of funds, even though they write about activities that require discretionary income.

There may be other activities you enjoy doing with a potential partner, such as day trips, touring museums, going to theme parks, skiing, dining out, concerts, and anything else that requires a checkbook or credit card. If this potential mate doesn't have the same desires or discretionary income, it's time to decide whether to continue cultivating this relationship or not.

Let's assume someone has the desire, but just doesn't have the finances. There can be many reasons for this. It could be they just didn't plan for retirement, or maybe they lost their nest egg because of a divorce, business loss, health crisis, hurricane, or other reasons beyond their control. Is there time for this person to recoup their losses and be a contributing partner? That's something you have to determine and what you're willing to do in the meantime.

If you're in your *golden years*, having a partner with the finances to do the same kinds of things you look forward to may be very important to you. Will you feel cheated or missed out on your dreams after years of working if you choose to stay with someone who's unable to do the things you want? *Be honest.*

Another alternative is to pay the other person's way. If you are able and willing, that's fine. Words of caution: Some people say they can't pay and will tap your finances until gone. Sorry, this alternative is not one I choose, with or without the finances.

Lessons Learned:
- Ask questions early to see if they will participate in the activities that you really want to do with a partner. If they hesitate, probe a little deeper to find out if it's because of finances. Be careful, because this is a very sensitive topic,

especially if someone doesn't have much discretionary income.

- Pay attention to hints made by a potential match concerning their discretionary income or lack thereof.
- If you are a frequent traveler, don't reveal all those trips taken because:
  o That conversation can be a bit overwhelming to a non-traveler.
  o It can give the wrong impressions of your finances and the amount of money you've spent traveling.
- If someone expects you to always pay for your food and drink, this is a red flag. However, I don't believe one person should *always* pay either. Everyone thinks differently, and couples should eventually discuss finances so you are both in agreement.
- If someone won't ever have the finances to do the things you really want to do, think about moving on so that you can avoid feeling resentful down the road. Don't let a pretty face cause you to ignore future issues.
- Don't be made to feel guilty because you planned for retirement and they didn't. On the flip side, refrain from making those that didn't plan, feel guilty. *Move on.*

20. Not so Heavenly

The following story is from a good friend who went on a date with a Rabi:

Clothing-Optional Rabi
My friend was asked out on a first date with someone she met online who was a rabbi. Seeing my friend is also Jewish, she thought he may have real possibilities. They had a lovely dinner with great conversation. After they finished eating, the Rabi asked her if she wanted to go to a disco. She wondered if discos still existed nowadays, especially in the area where they had dinner. He said there was one nearby and she could follow him in her car. She was curious, and away she went. She was led down a dirt road until they came to a place named Paradise Lakes.

As she told me her story, I thought the dirt road would have been enough for me to make a U-turn immediately. First, my friend didn't know for sure he was *really* a Rabi, and, second, down a lonely dirt road? Probably not a good idea on a first encounter with someone you just met. People tend to trust religious leaders. This could have turned out very badly for my friend.

They parked their cars and walked into a building, where she quickly found out it was a "clothing-optional" community. She was shocked at what she saw and even more shocked why a Rabi would take her there. He told her she didn't have to remove her clothes, as it was optional.

Oh, yeah, that would make me feel a lot more comfortable with him...*not*! I would wonder when he would start shedding. What an awkward situation that would be.

> *That was a big NO for her! Clothing-Optional Rabi insisted on giving her a tour of the facilities (naked people unavoidable).She tried to hide her horror at what she was exposed to (no pun intended). She finally asked him, "Why do you come here?"*

More importantly, why did he invite *her* there? I'm not sure why my friend didn't spin on her heals and find the quickest exit as soon as she realized where she had been taken. Perhaps it was curiosity or the fact that Clothing-Optional Rabbi was so charming and, let's not forget, religious.

> *He replied, "It's a way for me to get away from the expectations of my life."*

That's going from one end of the spectrum to the other. In the future, when I meet a Rabi or any other religious leader, I'll wonder if they are also a member of a clothing-optional community. That might be one of my first questions in the future, "How do you get away from the expectations of your life?"

I won't go into any more details of her visions that evening, because they would make you blush. My friend quickly excused herself and drove home with lasting memories etched in her head. And now I have those memories fixed in *my* brain!

Lessons Learned:
- On a first date, not advisable to follow someone to a place you are not familiar, especially down dark, rural roads.
- Don't assume that a religious man doesn't do or act like any other man might.

- It's okay to reject requests or suggested requests to change your lifestyle to accommodate a potential partner's wishes because you want them to like or date you.
- If you feel uncomfortable in your surroundings, it's okay to leave. Don't be persuaded to continue when you know this isn't the place for you. You don't have to be somewhere you don't want to be, or made to feel like you should.

21. No Backbone...No Money

Spineless Sam

I dated a down-to-earth, nice guy for several months named Sam. He was funny, liked to dance, go to different places, made me laugh, and enjoyed a nice glass of wine. He owned a tiny duplex in an artsy beach community, where he lived in one side and rented out the other.

When I met him, he was allowing a woman stay in the other side of his duplex for free because she had just left an abusive relationship. The adjoining door between units was usually open, and I could see her king-sized bed in the middle of the living room. She would just walk into his apartment at will. I told him this was a strange setup and a little uncomfortable for me, but it wasn't my house. He said it was only a temporary situation.

He kept talking about all the repairs he needed to make and stuff he had to get rid of to make his place a bit more habitable. It was a bit cluttered and very, very tiny. However, I discovered he was a great procrastinator. There were boards and bicycle parts strewn in the yard. Weeds were growing as tall as the bottoms of the windows. Parts of motorcycles were under a make-shift lean-to. There were several sheds in the back that definitely needed painting. The porch stretched across the entire back of the house. You couldn't walk from one end to the other because of all the stuff stacked from floor to ceiling: old magazines, newspapers, and boxes of who knows what.

After dating several months, Sam and I took a trip to Reno and northern California to visit his family and friends. Soon after that trip, the "lady moocher" had moved out, and an old friend of his had moved in. She seemed like a hippie from years ago, but was nice. However, he went from one moocher to another.

I started questioning the future of our relationship because of how he let people take advantage of him. The result was Spineless Sam not having the money to do the things that he wanted to do with me or to fix up his place. I'm a person who takes care of business, and I was seeing that Spineless conflicted with my values. I did speak to him about his situation, and he totally agreed with me. He said he would get sterner with his renters and get the money owed him as a landlord.

I was going to leave for a two-week trip to Minnesota and Wisconsin to visit relatives and decided not to ask Sam to join me. I figured he would be bored and probably couldn't afford to go anyway. While there, I unexpectedly bought property on a chain of lakes where I used to live. I flew back to Florida, packed up my car, and drove back to Minnesota to spend the summer—without telling Spineless Sam. By that time, I was feeling frustrated with him and his freeloading friends.

After I got to Minnesota, I felt bad and called Sam to see if he wanted to fly up and visit me. He responded by saying that he really couldn't afford the $200 airfare. That was it for me! I decided it was time to part ways, as it really bothered me that

Spineless Sam just didn't seem to have any backbone when it came to getting his rent money from people who just took advantage of him. Now it directly affected our relationship because he couldn't afford cheap airfare to come visit me—or hardly anything else, for that matter.

When I got back to Florida, I got a call from Sam. He told me he had moved into the house where his ex-wife had been living since they divorced five years earlier. She hadn't paid him any of the money he was owed, and now he was stuck with a house that was nearly destroyed. He had no money to fix it up. Not shocked with his sob story. Spineless Sam didn't have the money for the repairs because he still wasn't getting paid from his duplex renters. Again, not shocked.

I'm so glad I didn't stick with this guy! Sometimes nice guys do finish last. Even though I enjoyed his company, I wasn't willing to ride his train to nowhere.

Lessons Learned:
- Ask questions early on to see if they have an interest in traveling and can afford it—if that's important to you.
- Pay attention to conversations that tell you if they are good money managers. If not, and they aren't willing to take advice to make changes, decide to move on.
- If their living arrangements aren't in sync with yours, discuss this aspect with them and then decide whether you can put up with it or not.
  - Keep in mind that people are who they are, and they won't be changing any time soon, especially when over 50.

o   Understand your boundaries when it comes to what you are able to put up with long-term.

22. Just Plain Weird

Weird can be described as: *making no sense, strange, creepy, peculiar, bizarre, or a really uncomfortable feeling produced by someone's words or deeds.*

> **Babbling Bob's Profile** (verbatim)
> *"I'm a combo of seriousness and frivolity, often displaying a sober face that breaks into smile. A wide one too! While a conservative politically, I am quite liberal for my age when it comes to dress and physical appearance. Yet, I have been well grounded in God's Word—the anchor that has kept me for so many years—my reference to the real world; a world that has ups, downs, sadness, joy, triumph and disappointment. Can you relate to the human experience? It was never meant to be easy. I love Jordan B. Peterson's book 12 Rules For Life. He stands with the best of thinkers and can demolish the best liberal minds this world can offer. You Tube him if you would like; I promise it will keep your sanity in a world seeking to destroy itself. I too have recently written a novel called (REDACTED), and if you want to know how I think you should read it! A person's writing and artistic expression reveals something much deeper about them and provides answers to whether you can be compatible in relationship, be it friends or more. I am quite passionate about many things: colors, shapes, history, Israel, human touch and love. Like a fine wine, time has and still is teaching me about personalities; the ones that are healthy for*

relationships I desire. The good ones that refuse to control. The ones that understand that a thriving intimacy, both physically and emotionally, requires an atmosphere, a pasture in which to freely graze. That is where we discover each other's souls and true treasures. That is what we fall in love with and it grows over time. Finding joy in seeing the other fulfill their calling, their destiny and giving them preference. In the end it will be how we have treated others—have walked in love toward them. That includes neighbors and beyond into the realm of our husbands, wives and children, but maybe should not be in that order.

Say, let's pull the cork on that aged fine wine, and this time, this time, pour that seriousness and frivolity into two glasses so we can dance in the face of danger and rejoice at forces that are unable to overtake us. This end is just our beginning! Come with me?"

Gosh, there are so many moving parts in this profile it's difficult to dissect. I think that anyone reading this would feel exhausted, confused, cautious, turned off, and puzzled. I wonder what it would be like to actually meet this person and try to carry on a conversation that actually makes sense. For sure, I would need an interpreter. *"danger," pasture in which to freely graze,""Dance in the face of danger, "and "rejoice at forces unable to overtake us?"* He's in the Twilight Zone!

Lesson Learned:
- Read profiles with some insight into what they may be like in person.

146

- Beware of someone who writes in circles or says things that make you wonder what planet they're on.

Porno Paul
Paul said he was a retired police chief and now working the midnight shift as a hospital security guard.

I didn't want to know what city he was the police chief. Our communication quickly moved to texting on our personal phones.

The first day, and unexpectedly, he sent me a picture of him from the waist up taking a shower and lathering his hair when he got home after working the graveyard shift. Whoa!

He told me that he didn't expect me to return a picture "unless you want to."

No way! I declined the invite, wondering what might be coming next. I surely have seen enough to know that a stupid move on my part might end with my less-than-perfect body smeared all over the internet.

Moments later, I received a picture of him from the waist down with a small white towel covering his lower half. I must say, the picture showed a distinctive outline of what was under that towel and obviously what he had to offer me, with the message, "And before you ask, no, I am not excited under that towel."

In disbelief, I did not answer that text, contemplating what to say to him. You would think an ex-police chief wouldn't put himself in this kind of incriminating situation.

> *Before I had a chance to respond, I received another picture with a head-down shot of Porno Paul in his boxer shorts and the caption: "Getting ready to hit the hay! Of course, the boxers will come off LOL."*

Again, the shorts left little to one's imagination. Did he think I was going to jump in my car and rush over? Sad to say there are people on these sites who would do just that. I just wasn't one of them.

> *He didn't get the response he expected because I told him that he was a "bad boy" and thought the pictures were out of line.*

The texting and pictures stopped. It makes me wonder how far he would have gone with a little encouragement. My principles overruled my curiosity.

Lessons Learned:
- When nude or semi-nude photos appear uninvited, tell them it's not okay to send any more.
- People who send inappropriate photos to people they've never met are probably looking for a certain reaction. No reaction will likely give them permission to send more revealing photos.
- Don't let someone's occupation make it okay for them to do things that you know aren't appropriate.
- In retrospect, using the term "bad boy" could be taken as a compliment or a turn-on to some. Stronger verbiage

would have made a tougher statement toward showing my distaste for his unwanted photos and comments.
- DO NOT reciprocate with nude or semi-nude photos! Your reputation and future could be at stake.

Kinky Ken's Profile (verbatim)
"Sincere, honest, fun, positive. No substitute for communication, genuinely caring and understanding. Romantic and affectionate only when it is mutual and compatible. Pleasant and playful sense of humor is always fun. It could be as friends, it could be as dating, and it could be a sincere relationship. If at first you don't succeed...try 2nd base."

Ken caught my eye because of his brief but interesting profile. I sent him a message saying that I really liked what he wrote. However, I was curious what "2nd base" meant.

He responded right away, commenting about the things I had written. He actually read my profile and gave me a number of kudos. I was pleased he noticed I was a Virgo and that I was writing a book. He did ask me about the topic, and I responded by saying it was regarding snippets of my life.

I couldn't really tell him it was about online dating. In my experience, it's unusual for a man to notice that many specifics in a profile, so I was impressed.

Our messages were very interesting, and Ken seemed to be educated and used good grammar and punctuation. He told me that my life was "quite exceptional." Thanks for noticing!

We bantered back and forth with a little humor, giving information about our children and grandchildren. We started talking about golf, and then he sent a message saying, "There is an aspect within me that I rarely show…and I would like to share it with you, in sincerity…if that is okay with you?"

I thought he was talking about golf, but then Ken wrote, "The thing about golf is not what I wanted to share with you."

I replied, "Ok…I'm listening."

Kinky Ken said, "I believe I have shared with you that I do love to please…right? I do enjoy pleasing very much, deferring to a woman."

"Ok…I sense there is more," I responded hesitantly.

"Yes…in deferring to a woman…I prefer to do what she wants," Ken replied.

"And…?" I replied.

"You may or may not know of such," wrote Ken.

All of a sudden it hit me, and the light bulb flashed on.

I asked, "Correct me if I'm wrong, but are you trying to say you are looking for a dominant/submissive relationship?"

While he was responding, I quickly searched the internet for dominant/submissive relationships, trying to find something positive about it. I just had visions of being dressed in black leather with spurs and Kinky Ken dressed like a baby. It wasn't a pretty picture, or one that I wanted to act out in real life.

"Yes, but not in a negative manner of it…only in the caring, positive and loving type," he answered.

"Guess I like a 50/50 relationship, Ken," I responded.

"Of that, I totally understand…I really do," he answered. "I just wanted to be honest with you…as it isn't something I share often and at the same time, I do have very high regards for you…and truly I understand your preferences."

I said, "Thank you for being honest and upfront with me."

"Thank you for allowing me to be truthful," Kinky Ken answered back.

We wished each other a Merry Christmas and good luck.

Bummer! Except for Kinky Ken's confession, he seemed to have all the attributes I was looking for in a man. Better to find this out early before I'm handed a whip or asked to gag him with a ball and squirt him with coconut oil.

Lessons Learned:
- Be honest and upfront with potential matches so energy and time isn't wasted.
- Pay attention to phrases and words that could give you clues of issues or raise red flags.

- When you learn things about someone's lifestyle that's different from yours, it's time to make the decision to stay or leave.

23. More Than I Wanted to Know

Tacky Wacky Jack

About the time I starting using dating sites more extensively, I began communicating with Jack, who said he lived in Florida. I don't remember specifics about his profile, except that his photos were blurry. He seemed like an okay guy who wanted to take me out for dinner. At the time, I was in Minnesota for the summer and heading back to Florida soon. I agreed to go out with him when I returned.

While talking to Jack on my trip back, he confessed he really lived in Kentucky but visited Florida often on vacations. I was thinking he was probably searching for someone from Florida so he could vacation more often with a free place to stay. I wasn't pleased about his lack of honesty in his profile, but still agreed to meet him for dinner because I hadn't had an "interview" or a dinner invite in awhile. Just being honest!

By the time I returned to Florida, Jack was already there on his vacation and was ready to make good on his dinner invitation. We agreed on the restaurant, and he said he would pick me up. I quickly said, "No, thank you. I'll meet you there."

No way that I'm giving him my address or allowing him to pick me up at my house and riding in his car, considering we've never met! That's how you end up on *Dateline* or *20/20*.

We met and had a pleasant dinner at a nice riverfront restaurant in a very touristy area. Toward the end of our meal, I noticed with each topic of conversation, he interjected sexual comments. Then he told me that he didn't date much but tried to keep his "parts" in working order. By the end of our dinner, he had told me all about his masturbation schedule! Yes, you heard me correctly. On the inside, I was stunned! On the outside, I remained quiet and expressionless, not displaying my horror at what I was hearing.

Tacky Wacky Jack was calm and very matter-of-fact about his sexual confession, and I tried hard to act like I wasn't in shock. I just listened without commenting, but thought...*What guy talks about this topic on a first date or second, or third, or ever? Am I a prude? Where do these people come from, where they discuss this with someone they just met? Please, let this night be over soon.*

Tacky Wacky walked me back to my car after dinner. He then asked, "Do you want to come back to my hotel?"

"No!"

"You don't have to worry about me because I won't lay a hand on you, I promise," Tacky Wacky Jack pleaded.

I couldn't help but think that could be true, but he may want me to watch *him* lay a hand on *himself!* *No, thank you!* What makes a person think they should reveal such personal information to a perfect stranger? I'm thinking Tacky Wacky Jack thought I would be impressed that, at his age, he was still able to perform. *Not on the first date while eating my dessert!*

Even without the sexual conversation, going to someone's hotel room is a big no-no...whether you like them or not. In this case, there was no chemistry of any kind. I couldn't get other thoughts out of my head.

I got in my car and drove home, relieved and thankful the evening was over. Later, I couldn't get the vision out of my head of what Tacky Wacky Jack might be doing back at his hotel room. Erase! Brain bleach!

We all want to feel like we're adults and can handle sexual conversations. We act like it doesn't shock us, when, in fact, it does! I didn't want to come across like a scolding mother or a naïve prude. I knew the evening would be short and that I would never see this person again.

Lessons Learned:
- *Never* have someone pick you up in their vehicle on the first several encounters. Always meet in a public place, like I did in this situation.
- When someone reveals a sexual confession, and you're not comfortable with it, calmly put them in their place with a polite change of subject. If that doesn't work, be more direct and tell them you don't appreciate the sexual conversation, or just leave.
- Staying quiet sends the wrong message, because they may think you are totally okay with the topic. It gives them permission to keep saying further tasteless conversations to you and others.

24. Across the Country

This message was sent to me after I responded to this individual's "Hi" message by telling him there was too much distance between us to develop a relationship. Not a lot of thought went into his original message, because it was a "flirt" response.

> **Long-Distance Larry**
> *"What a loss to have missed that experience by limiting yourself to a certain number of miles...Well, I will enjoy personal email conversation...Let's see if we have anything in common, we can email. If you never take the chance, then how will you ever find the right one?"*

Long-Distance Larry lived in Los Angeles and I lived in Florida. Of the 3.9 million people living in Los Angeles, half of whom are women, he thinks the *right one* may be in Florida? I guess he won't find out.

I have received many messages from men who say they want to get to know me, but they live across the United States and even in other countries. It's too difficult and expensive to cultivate a relationship when you have to fly to meet. These types of requests make me question if they are real people. I know there are some couples who have met online and cultivated successful long-distance relationships, but unless you have your own plane and a lot of discretionary income, the odds aren't in your favor.

Remember, many profiles aren't real. I am *very* skeptical about these types of messages and usually do not respond.

I recall sending a message to someone who looked interesting and lived only 40 *minutes* away. He responded that he didn't want a *long-distance* relationship. Wow! I drive farther than that for a round of golf or lunch. I guess everyone has their own perspective on distance.

I know a woman who traveled to India by herself to meet someone she had met online. That's just plain crazy! She turned it into a buying trip, just for a reason to go there, but that was a really risky and expensive way to meet someone for the first time. The relationship didn't go anywhere when they met, but she did get home safely. I'm a risk taker, but this situation gives that a whole new meaning.

Lessons Learned:
- Making a determination of whether you want to continue cultivating a long-distance relationship is a matter of preference. Ask yourself these questions:
  o Is this person real? Find this out before your heart gets broken.
  o Do they want to spend time getting to know you before jumping into an airplane?
  o Do you have the funds to travel to see them?
  o Do they have the funds to travel to see you?
  o Is either of you willing to relocate if the relationship gets to that point?
  o Would you be comfortable having them stay at your home the first time you meet? Is this ever a good idea? A hotel is the best option.
  o Are they a trustworthy prospect? Remember, trust takes time to build.
  o Are you being rushed into this relationship or feeling uncomfortable in *any* way?
- Safety is first and foremost. When you first meet, even after a relationship has formed, make it at a public place

and make sure a friend or family member knows where you are and who you are with.

- Don't put yourself in a vulnerable situation where you are alone and in an unfamiliar place.
- Check this person out on the internet using information they mentioned in your conversations. Research can reveal information that can help you determine whether this person is truthful, real, or has secrets.
- If they're respectful of you, they will honor your request to stay at a hotel the first time you meet. If not, rethink your invitation.
- Above all else, use your best judgment, because your life may depend on it. This person could be the love of your life or Jack/Jane the Ripper.

25. Booty Callers

All Caps Karl (verbatim)
"GOODMORNIN' SWEET,SEXY NICO---OR IS THAT UR PUPS NAME? U R EXACTLY WHAT EVERY GUY IS LOOKIN' 4 SUGAR...A SEXY, GORGEOUS & SEXUALLY EXCITIN' WOMAN...U MEAN I'M NOT WHAT U R LOOKIN' 4! GOOD LUCK& HAVE FUN SEXY...BYE BYE"

The message above was written in response to my telling him that I didn't think we were a match. *Call me crazy to pass this up!*

Nooner Nick
One of the first responses I received after signing up on a dating site was from someone who sounded very interesting. We talked on the phone that same day. However, it wasn't long into that call before he asked me if he could come over before I left for work in two hours. I told him "no." I didn't even know him! He kept insisting, until I just ended the conversation.

It didn't take a rocket scientist to figure out his agenda.

Believe it or not, there are websites for the *booty callers*, such as Onlinebootycall.com, Affairhub.com, Grindr, BeNaughty.com, and more. Some sites have reputations for matching users exclusively for the sake of *hooking up*, and if you're green to online dating, you might not know which ones they are, even though someone may recommend a site to you. I signed up for Tinder at a friend's recommendation, and my granddaughter was in disbelief when she heard about it. She's been on dating sites and shared that it probably wasn't the kind of site her grandma should be on. It's a crazy world when your granddaughter gives you online dating advice.

Tinder and Plenty of Fish (POF) have reputations for containing a lot of *brief encounter* prospects. However, there is the potential of encountering booty callers on most online dating sites—even the Christian ones. That's why a person has to know what they are looking for and how to weed out what they don't want based on clues they read or hear.

People who are interested in hookup dating should go to the websites designed for this purpose and stay off the serious dating sites.

If only.

Lessons Learned:
- Read dating site reviews before signing up.
- Make your intentions known in your profile and messages. Ask questions to confirm the intentions of your prospects.
- When reviewing profiles and messages, read between the lines for hidden meanings.
- Don't let yourself be bullied into doing something you're not comfortable doing.
- If you don't want the advances of someone, tell them to look elsewhere and move on.
- You can also block people and/or report them to the dating site.

26. Separating the Wheat from the Chaff

What are you looking for in a partner? Before you sign up on a dating site, make a list of those attributes and list them as: Required, Nice to Have, and Deal breakers. If you know what you want and don't want, you can more easily choose the people you want to learn more about just by what they write in their profile or in their first couple messages.

There's an old adage: "You can't judge a book by its cover." As mentioned earlier, it's just amazing the strange pictures people post to get attention. The *first impression* is formed from that main picture. The second is formed when you actually click on their profile to learn more about a person. Keep in mind, many times people choose the wrong main picture, when other photos in their profile may tell a very different story.

Let's say you've already decided that the picture piqued your interest enough to take a further look. From that point, you are searching for *your* criteria about each match. We all have different requirements for a potential partner, and there are many questions that roll around in our heads when deciding to pursue someone, especially on dating sites.

The rest of this chapter contains a number of questions to help you make a determination as to whether to pursue someone or to move on. Your past experiences may necessitate additional questions to add to my list.

Questions to ask when reviewing potential matches:
- ➤ Does the main picture have enough appeal to go further into their profile?
- ➤ Do you have enough in common?
- ➤ Do you feel any negative vibes or feel uncomfortable when reading a profile?
- ➤ Does the profile pique your interest enough to send a message?
- ➤ Does at least one picture show a smile? Preferably, the majority of the pictures include a smiling face.
- ➤ Are there anger issues? This is based on the way they write their profile (examples include bashing past relationships or listing a lot of negatives).
- ➤ Do you feel uplifted or excited after reading a profile, or do you feel more downbeat and unenthusiastic?

Questions to ask when exchanging messages:
- ➤ Are your messages answered, and in a timely manner?
- ➤ Do they sound like they're genuinely interested in you?
- ➤ Do they sound positive and upbeat? Do you detect any anger?
- ➤ Are *gushy* words used in their messages, such as "beautiful," "gorgeous," and, "baby?" How does that make you feel? Are you okay with that?
- ➤ Are there some alternative activities you find interesting and would like to try?
- ➤ Do they try to find out more about you, or just talk about themselves?

Questions after the first *interview*:
- ➤ Do they meet you on time, and does it bother you if they don't?
- ➤ Is the conversation monopolized by talking about them?
- ➤ Are you treated respectfully in words and deeds?
- ➤ Is general attitude and outlook compatible with yours?

- Do they seem interested in your life, family, future goals, etc.?
- Do they have or think about future goals or plans regarding how they want to spend the rest of their life? How do these fit into your life plans?
- Perhaps the first time you meet, one or both of you may be nervous. Do you need a second *interview* to see if perceived negative traits were just because of nervousness?
- If chemistry is important to you, do you feel any attraction, or does that determination require another get-together?
- If spirituality is important to you, did you address this in your conversations? Did you like the answers?
- Is this person into religion more or less than you? Can you deal with that?
- If religious or political discussions are brought up, what are your reactions to the discussion? Positive or negative?
- Does the interview end with you feeling good about yourself and future possibilities with this person?

Questions to ask after several dates:
- When you're ready, are they willing to meet your family and friends, or do they just want you all to themselves? How does that make you feel? Are you feeling separated from your friends and family?
- Do your friends and family give you a *thumbs-up*? If they have reservations about this new person in your life, do you value their concerns because they may see something you overlooked?
- Do you start making excuses and defending bad behavior?
- Are you seeing any issues that need to be addressed? Are these deal breakers, or can they be resolved easily? Realize that if it's a character flaw that you don't like, chances are this won't change. It doesn't hurt to try and

see if communicating your concern actually makes a difference. By this stage in our lives, what you see is what you get.

➢ Do you feel you can easily bring up your questions, concerns, or issues, or do you feel it may jeopardize the relationship?

➢ When talking about this person to your friends, are you relating mostly positive attributes or negative ones? This may indirectly show your true thoughts about this relationship.

➢ Were you honest in sharing what you are looking for in a relationship? Does this person share your feelings?

➢ Do you honestly feel this person matches what you are looking for without any major red flags?

Based on this self-assessment, you should be able to separate the wheat from the chaff. Of course, *your* specific goals, desires, deal breakers, and interests will dictate your decisions. If your intuition is telling you this isn't the right person, don't waste your time and energy by trying to make it work. Remember *my* lessons learned throughout this book.

Don't compromise because you don't want to go through the process again and again, or because you don't want to spend your life alone. If you do, it's because you've made that conscious choice. Not everyone is the right person. Trust your gut. You want to feel good and excited about your choice.

27. Other Ways to Meet Your Mate

Like the song, *"Looking for Love in All the Wrong Places"*

–*Johnny Lee, 1980*

I have a great idea! Everyone should have a chip implanted in their forehead that lights up different colors…blue for single, red for married, and yellow for being in a committed relationship. This information is crucial when you see someone with potential, so he/she doesn't get away without making a connection because you didn't know they were available. It would save time, energy, and the embarrassment of an angry wife or girlfriend knocking you to the ground for striking up a conversation with *their* man. However, it could be *shame on you* for not!

When I first divorced back in the early '80's, there were no cell phones or internet. How did we manage? The dating scene for singles was quite different. Today, people spend hours surfing the internet for information *and* love. However, there are other ways to meet your mate *other than* online dating that are less risky and that may be of interest to you.

Perhaps you need to put your eggs in more than one basket. *Clichés seem to be inherent to someone from the Midwest.*

Below are some additional ideas to help in your search for a special someone:

- *Personal Ads.* Newspaper personal ads were the method used pre-internet to meet someone and are still used in some local papers today. You are allowed to write only a few words about yourself and what you are looking for. That was difficult for me, as I recall, because I had so many admirable qualities worth sharing. *Ahem.*

These little blurbs would be published as a blind ad in a special Section of the paper, titled *Personal Ads*, where you were given a number. If someone was interested, they would contact the newspaper, giving them your ad number. The newspaper in turn contacted you with their phone number. I can even remember some of those blind dates today—this one was quite memorable.

Cheap Charlie
I recall setting up a dinner date with a man named Charlie many years ago in response to one of those ads in the newspaper. He showed up in a really nice, restored, green-and-white, shiny 1956 Chevy with dice hanging from the rearview mirror. After all, it was in the early '80's!

I ordered a small salad, thinking it would be easy to eat and talk simultaneously. I guess Charlie was really hungry, because he ordered a salad, steak, baked potato, and dessert.

What? No appetizer!

The conversation involved the normal question-and-answer dialogue of getting to know one another. I liked his look—a trimmed mustache and huskier build; plus, he could carry on a relevant conversation.

When the waitress handed Cheap Charlie the bill, he said to me, "We can just split the bill, right?"

This guy ordered a full meal, and I ate a side salad. How did that constitute splitting? My impression of Cheap Charlie changed in that moment. It was my first blind date, and I was a bit timid. So, I paid half and figured I would not be seeing this *cheapo* again.

Today, I would have handled this situation much differently by saying we should go "Dutch." That was a great first date—until it wasn't. It turned out to be a total waste of my time and money.

After that, I only responded to a few of these ads because they really weren't productive. Plus, you had no idea what the other party looked like before meeting, and I'm not crazy about that kind of a surprise.

Recently, a friend, who had not dated for 10 years since her husband passed away, told me she had answered several personal ads in a local paper. Until then, I didn't even know they still existed.

This is her story.

Dancing Dan

My friend answered an ad from someone who wanted a dance partner because she really missed that in her life. That was exactly what she was searching for.

They have been dancing together ever since, and he's always showing her new dance moves. She's enjoying the dancing friendship. To date, this relationship has been primarily for dancing and dinners together as good friends. She's not sure if it will be any more than that, but is totally okay with this arrangement for now.

Before Dancing Dan, I helped this same friend set up a profile on Plenty of Fish (POF). However, she wasn't on this site very long, because she didn't have much success, and she thought it was taking too long to find someone of interest. She's off POF and is still dancing the nights away with Dancing Dan.

- *Bars/Dance Halls.* Again, the dating scene is different today than when I was in my 30s and 40s. You don't see many single men out on a Friday or Saturday night sitting at the bar waiting to meet someone. There are bars like that, but I wouldn't frequent them.

There used to be a lot of local bars with great dancing bands near where I lived, but not today. You have to drive a long way from my locale to find one. I know there are late-night venues in my area, which the younger generation frequent. However, the time they're going out, I'm thinking about how comfortable my pillow looks. Besides, a cougar is one thing but robbing the cradle is quite another.

I go out almost every Friday night with friends, and I see few single men my age. I admit, when I'm out with three to six people, we probably appear to be a closed group. If someone were interested, they probably would not want to interrupt our conversations or risk being embarrassed. Plus, we usually go early to catch the happy-hour specials and then we're on our way home. Sad, but true!

A suggestion when you are out is to limit the number of people who are in your group. Two people are ideal. I'm reassessing how many of us go out together, and I'm paying more attention to the clientele. Unfortunately, there isn't much clientele to pay attention to. Where are they?

Where do they go? Do they just stay home watching sports and old westerns? Surfing the dating sites?

One reason people aren't out like they used to be is the fear of driving after a drink or two. Local law enforcement is much more proactive today compared to many years ago. It's a different time.

Many bars and restaurants have guitar music or other listening music for the patrons. If there were dancing music, our opportunities would be very different and popular. Most of us go home after happy hour because nothing is going on. I've been looking into more local venues with music since I changed locations. I think I need to put myself out there more, even if I have to go there alone.

Another tip I learned a long time ago is that sitting at the bar is more conducive to starting up a conversation with the people around you, rather than sitting at a table away from the bar. People are less threatened striking up a conversation when they are at the bar because they have a reason to be there, and there isn't any risk involved, like there might be walking up to a table of people. Strategically find your seat at the bar.

- *Referrals.* These are the best and preferred way to meet your mate because someone you know has vouched for his/her character and qualities. I have told my married friends, "I take referrals." However, people seem to be leery of setting up blind dates for their friends. They are afraid friendships may be jeopardized if things don't work out. All I can do is plant the seed in case they befriend someone who may be a good prospect to introduce to their single friend.

Misjudged-Me Fran

One time I had a married co-worker who said she had the "perfect man" for me and that he was about my age. Fran sent me his picture, and I was a bit surprised, because he looked a lot older than me. However, I didn't want to judge him by his picture alone, and maybe I look at myself in the mirror with rose-colored glasses.

Fran eagerly reported he had money and was able to travel and more. Oh, yes, she said he even drove an expensive car—as if that would make a big impression. He lived in Minnesota, where I had resided for 30 years, but now I lived in Florida.

She told him about me, and he was very anxious to meet. He would fly down to Florida whenever was good for me, so we could get to know one another. He was very open to spending time in the sunny South.

Then Misjudged-Me Fran dropped a bombshell! He had a history of prostate cancer, which left him with sexual dysfunction. He told her if it was an issue for me, he would do something about it. Misjudged-Me told him, "That wouldn't matter to Sandy." When she told me this, I exclaimed, "What are you thinking? Of course, it matters to me! Even at my age, I still would like everything working, at least to start with."

It's different when you have been with your mate for a long time and this situation occurs, and I know it is not uncommon. I just didn't want to start a new relationship knowing that this was what I had to look forward to—or not look forward to! Call me selfish.

- *Singles Groups.* The first thing I did after my second divorce was join a national singles golf organization that had a chapter in Tampa Bay. At that time, there were over two hundred members in the chapter. Wow! I thought this will be a great place to meet the man of my dreams—who also loves to golf.

  I am still in this group today, with lots of friends. I soon figured out that if you dated someone in the group and the relationship went sour, one of you probably was going to leave the group, and I didn't want that to be me. The two men I did date both boogied, and I never saw them again.

  If I were secretly interested in someone, they quickly got scooped up by someone else. I would rather develop a relationship outside of the group. I've made many long-term friends and stay for that reason. There have been many marriages between members in this organization. So, I've seen how a singles group can be very successful.

  There are many singles dance groups in your area to check out also. I used to attend some of these events, but found them to be a bit of a meat market. Perhaps I should try them again to see if things have changed. However, there aren't as many as in the past.

- *Meet Up Groups.* Organizations where people have similar interests are a great way to meet someone, and they don't have to necessarily be in singles groups. This is where those colored chips would come in handy that I suggested earlier! If you haven't joined a meet-up group, you are really missing out on great opportunities to meet people with similar interests.

  There is a meet up group for almost any type of activity you can think of. These groups are in major cities all over the United States. Also, anyone can start one of their own, if you can't find one of interest in your location. They are very popular, and many don't cost anything to try out. Although, check this out before signing up with a group. The word recently is Meet Up will start charging when you RSVP for an event (Meetup.com).

There is a new site called GetMeetingStar.com. They are an alternative group for meeting people and attending events. Its 100 percent free for groups up to 250 members, with no limit to events and no RSVP charges. I'll be checking these groups out in the near future.

If you don't like one, try another. This should be at the top of your to do list.

- *Airplanes and Airports.* I used to travel every week for work and thought for sure I would meet the man of my dreams sitting next to me in an airplane. Nope…didn't happen—not yet anyway. Most who I spoke to were married, and others weren't into conversation. However, one never knows who's sitting next to you. Saying "Hello" could be the start of something special. Therefore, being friendly on an airplane is always a plus.

- *Golf/Sports.* As much as I golf, I was sure I would meet a love interest at the 19th hole or when I was paired with unknown golf partners at out-of-town courses. I've met a lot of great golfers, but none that were long-lasting love interests. When golfing frequently with groups of friends, one would think that there would be single men loitering in the pub after playing a round. Maybe when we stop at the 19th, we look intimidating as a group. Men are usually in groups, and don't usually have an interest in striking up extra conversations with a group of women golfers. Could it be because they are all married, or too exhausted?

Maybe we look like pro-golfers, and they are intimidated? Remember...you don't know who's around the next tee box.

Perhaps you are a football, basketball, or other sports team fan...or not. Many places have special events going on during games where there are a lot of people in attendance having a good time and who are open to conversation. Take a friend and attend one, and you are almost guaranteed to meet people.

- *Grocery Store.* Some people have had success squeezing the mangos and cantaloupes in the produce department. I have heard this tale, but have never known anyone who has found their mate in this venue. How long does a person spend their time squeezing and strategically wandering the produce department looking for single-looking men lingering? Maybe someone will ask if I know how to tell when the cantaloupes are ripe. Perhaps I should be asking that question to get a conversation going? That's a bit bold, even for me. Keep your eyes open for opportunities.

- *Walking Your Dog or Llama.* This could be a great way to find another animal lover. People walk their dogs several times a day every day. I have met a number of people walking my dog, but not one that asked for my phone number—yet! Find a well-traveled trail or dog park and go there on a regular basis. This may give someone the idea they can strike up a conversation on the second or third time. Everyone likes compliments on their pets and it's an easy way to meet someone.

- *Living in 55+ Communities.* You already know the people are in your same age bracket. My last three places of residence have been in over-55 communities where there were a number of eligible men, but mostly a lot older than me or already taken. There are usually more single women than men so you have to act fast and not be bashful. It's a double plus if you're a golfer and live in a 55+ golf development.

I was asked out for New Year's Eve by an 89-year-old neighbor in my 55+ community. I didn't want to give him or others the wrong idea, so I declined his invite. *I did feel bad later about not going.*

Consider living in a development where there is ample opportunity to meet someone. There should be a lot of activities available, such as singles groups, cards or sports onsite, a golf course, or whatever you enjoy. An onsite bar and restaurant are great places to meet your neighbors. I don't have those amenities where I now live, but wished I did. I'm thinking about starting a golf league to meet new people in my community which isn't 55+. There is a good mix of age groups and it may have opportunities for a *cougar*.

- *Restaurants.* Frequenting a nearby restaurant may be a good way to meet someone, especially if it's close to where you live. Many single people my age eat out a lot. Mr. Right could be sitting at the table next to you. Be the first to strike up a conversation. What do you have to lose?

- *Churches or Synagogues.* This venue for meeting someone has been promoted by people forever. I actually did meet and date someone from the same church I attended years ago. It can be a place to meet people of your religion. However, don't think that because they are church-goers, they are without issues.

I wouldn't propose joining or attending a church/synagogue for the *sole* purpose of meeting someone. If you do, it's in the deceitful category. Just keep your mind and eyes open at your place of worship. If you know the pastor, it wouldn't hurt to let them know you're open to meeting single people, because they know their flock. Many churches have singles groups, too. Check them out.

- *The Gym.* Today, more people our age are going to a gym to keep fit. Most singles are looking for someone who cares about how they look. If you're going to a gym, you *must* want to look and feel your best. The gym is an excellent place to easily strike up conversations about fitness, help with a machine, or just chit chat in general. Look at it this way—you are getting fit while keeping your eyes open. With Silver Sneakers available to the over 62 generation, it doesn't even cost you anything to be a member.

There are many more places where a single and active person can meet someone. You have to always be prepared for that moment by wearing a smile and keeping your ears and eyes open. Don't be afraid to strike up a conversation.

If you're not sure if someone is single, use a question to see what your next move should be. Example: *"Doesn't your wife/husband like to golf?"* Or *"Is your wife making you a nice home-cooked meal after your hard day of golfing?"* Be creative and adapt your question to the situation.

28. My Future

Some people tell me, "You need to compromise more," "You're too fussy," or similar comments. I don't pay much attention to those words, because I'm very happy with my life. I know what I want and don't want. I'm just particular on how I want to spend the rest of my life. Of course, there's always the possibility *the one* will show up one day and sweep me off my feet...or maybe not. I'm okay with that, but I do think there will be a special person in my life in the future.

I've learned so much more about myself throughout this writing journey and from the online dating mistakes I've made along the way. The following are *my most important* lessons learned:

> ➤ How to spot would-be scammers earlier when communicating with someone new.
> ➤ Use available sites to verify email addresses if there are red flags by using websites such as: www.peoplelooker.com/email_lookup/email_records www.scamomatic.com
> ➤ Early in conversations, I'll use onomatopoeia words (words and phrases that imitate sounds, e.g., sizzle, cuckoo, hmmm) to determine if I'm talking to a real person or a bot.
> ➤ Keep safety as the main factor when making decisions. I will not *ever* let someone bully me into going somewhere or doing something I'm uncomfortable with.
> ➤ I'll express myself earlier and more clearly in a relationship about things I don't like. I'll stop inappropriate behavior *as* it occurs.

- ➤ If I'm uncomfortable during a conversation, I'll change the subject in a way that lets the other person knows he's being inappropriate. If it continues, I'll leave.
- ➤ When dating a widower, I'll ask better questions about his readiness to be in a relationship and watch for nonverbal signs he isn't ready.
- ➤ If someone I meet has a physical disability, I won't ignore it. I'll say in a sensitive way that I would like to know more about that aspect of their life when they're ready to talk about it.
- ➤ I'll refrain from talking too much about my travels or topics that don't focus on the other person. First, focus on him, and then, myself. The most interesting topic of conversation for most people is themselves.
- ➤ After thinking and writing about the other ways to meet someone, I will definitely act on those ideas as soon as I've finished writing this book.

I have a very fulfilled and active life and don't *require* a partner. I believe that marriage or a full-time relationship may not be best for me. It would, however, be nice to have someone who would be there for me, share stories, and enjoy life's experiences and intimate moments.

I've learned to accept myself as a special person and to enjoy all my good friends and family. I'll carry on my search for that special partner, but won't feel like I've failed if I don't. I will, at the same time, keep accomplishing my life goals and experiencing the world.

Even though I have not yet found *Mr. Right*, I have found something so unexpected...*this book*! Who knows where this will lead me, or to whom?

29. Your Future

Perhaps you have your own stories. What are your *Lessons Learned*? Hopefully, it will be a much shorter list after learning from my experiences and putting them into action.

Being safe is more than locking your car doors at night. It means being aware. Remember...people aren't always who they pretend to be and may take advantage of someone who *appears* to be vulnerable. If you're feeling uncomfortable about a situation, trust your gut and take measures to remove yourself from those situations or don't get into them in the first place.

This book has given you valuable tips on what to watch for when using online dating sites to keep you from being fooled by scammers. It may save you unnecessary heartache and financial ruin.

You are now armed with more tools in your tool belt. You are ready to highlight yourself as a person worthy of the kind of partner you desire and deserve. This book should enhance your online dating journey.

At times, I'm aware this book doesn't shed a positive light on the online dating scene. However, even if a relationship doesn't last a lifetime, a person can take away the positive aspects and learn from the negatives. It doesn't matter if you're young, over 50, or even 70. Keep in mind that not one of us is perfect.

Lastly, don't let finding a partner monopolize your life. Your own personal interests should be developed and enjoyed, keeping you motivated and loving life.

Success to you and be safe!

References

Allied Market Research. "Online Dating Services Market Outlook-2025."
www.alliedmarketsearchcon/online-dating-services-market

Arch. "A Deep Look at Online Dating Statistics". Sept 27, 2019
www.techjunkie.com/online=dating-statistics

Bahn, Clare. "How to Spot Fake Online Profiles." Nov 15, 1019.
www.onlineprofilepros.com/spot-fake-online-profiles

Brooks, Amber. "21 Amazing Online Dating Statistics-the Good, Bad &
Weird". 2020. www.datingadvice.com/online-dating-statistics

Brown, Dalvin. "Dating Sunday: The busiest day of the year for online
Dating is Jan 6." Jan 5, 2019. www.usatoday.com/story/news/
2019/01/05/dating-Sunday-how-stand-out

Carson, Erin. "Here are the photos you should use on your online dating
profile." www.cnet.com/news/photos-you-should-use-on-
your-online-dating-profile.

Clement, J."Online Dating in the United States-Statistics & Facts". 2020.
www.statista.com/statistics/most-popular-dating-apps-by-
audience-size-usa.

CNET.com. "Plenty of Fish". Jan 22, 2020.
www.cnet.com/pictures/best-datimg-apps/11

Consumer Rankings. "Our Top 5 Senior Picks of 2020."
www.consumer-rankings.com/senior-dating

Dating Sites Preview.com. "Online Dating Statistics & Facts."
www.datingsitesreviews.com/staticpages/index.php?page=
online-dating.

De Naoum, Kat. "The Best Dating Sites for Older Adults Looking for Love
Later in Life." Dec. 20, 2019. www.womansworld.com/posts/inspiration/17-
best-dating-sites-for-over-50.

Florida, Richard. "The Cities with the Most Singles." Feb 14, 2019.
www.citylab.com/life/2019/02/valentines-day-single-dating-best-cities-find

"The Geography of Online Dating.'" Apr 16, 2019.
www.citylab.com/life/2019/04/online-dating-sites-looking-for-love-near-me

Holt, Brianna. "The First Sunday in January is the Biggest Day of Online
Dating all Year." Dec, 2019. www.qz.com/177792/the-
best-day-to-be-active-on-dating-apps.

Knight, Will. "Talking to a bot." July 18, 2018. www.technologyreview.com/
611655/how-to-tell-if-youre-talking-to-a-bot.

Matthews, Hayley. "27 Online Dating Statistics & What They Mean for the

Future of Dating." www.datingnews.com/industry-trends/online-dating-statistics what-they-mean.

Mayer, Brittany. "11 Tips for Having the Best "Online Dating Photos"—(For Your Profile)." Apr 19, 2017 www.datingadvice.com/online-dating/online-dating.

Murray, Megan. "How to Choose the Best Online Dating Photo." May 15, 2017. www.zoosk.com/date-mix/online-dating-advice.

Papa, Ashley. "9 Ways Over 50 Dating Sites Differ From Their All Ages Counterparts." Oct 17, 2019. www.zoosk.com/date-mix/online-dating-advice.

Paul, Kari. "As Alleged-$46 M online-dating scams show, lonely-hearts are The biggest target for scam artists in America." Aug 24, 2019 www.marketwatch.com/story/love-is-biggest-scam-in-america-2019

Rouch, Joseph. "How To Tell If You're Talking to a Bot: The Complete Guide to Chatbots." Jan 22, 2017. www.talkspace.com/blog/How-to-tell-if-youre-talking-to-a-bot.

ScamWatch.com. "Dating & Romance." Feb, 2020 www.scamwatch.gov.au/types-of-scam/dating-romance

Seal, Kelly. "New study finds people don't like typos in dating profiles." Nov 28, 2019. www.dadtingsitesreviews.com/article.php?story=study-finds-people-don't-like-typos.

Statista. "Most Popular Online Dating Apps in U.S. as of Sep, 2019." www.statista.com/statistics/most-popular-dating-apps-by-audience-size-usa.
"Online Dating Worldwide". 2020 www.statista.comn/outlook/372/1001/online-dating/worlwide

Statistic Brain Institute. (Graphics) 2018 www.facebook.com/statisticbrain/photos

Thotlam, Isabel. "Online Dating Statistics You Should Know." www.eharmony.com/online-dating-statistics.

Top10.com. "The Best Online Dating Sites of 2020." www.top10bestdatingsites.com/comparison

Vogels, Emily A. "10 Facts about Americans and online dating." 2020 www.pewresearch.org/fact-tank/2020

CPSIA information can be obtained
at www.ICGtesting.com
Printed in the USA
FSHW010021240620

9 780578 631998